STEP BY STEP
Using
SuperCalc 3
on the
Amstrad PC

Using SuperCalc 3 on the Amstrad PC

Second Edition

P.K. McBride

Heinemann London

Heinemann Professional Publishing Ltd
22 Bedford Square, London WC1B 3HH

LONDON   MELBOURNE   JOHANNESBURG   AUCKLAND

First published by Newtech Books Ltd 1987
First published by Heinemann Professional Publishing Ltd 1987

©Heinemann Professional Publishing Ltd 1987

British Library Cataloguing in Publication Data
McBride,P.K.
Using SuperCalc3 on the Amstrad PC
– (Step by Step)
1. SuperCalc3 (Computer program)
2. Amstrad PC (Computer)
I Title   II Series
005.36'5   HF5548.4.S86

ISBN 0 434 91221 2

Designed by John Clark and Associates, Ringwood, Hampshire

Printed in the UK by HGA Printing Co. Ltd, Brentford, Middlesex

Contents

5

Contents

PART ONE

Getting started

■ SECTION 1
Introducing SuperCalc3

SuperCalc was one of the first electronic spreadsheets to be produced and has established itself as a firm favourite in the business computing world. SuperCalc3, the full-feature version now being marketed for the Amstrad PCs will, no doubt, extend its popularity even further. Its key facilities are so easy to understand and its operation so simple that it is possible to get useful work out of it within an hour of first starting, yet it has the capacity to handle the most complex and sophisticated applications.

Like all spreadsheets, SuperCalc3 is, in essence, a large grid of boxes, or cells, in which you can write text, numbers or formulae that will process those numbers. It is a general-purpose tool — a combination notepad, reference table and calculator — that can be used in an almost unlimited number of ways. Financial modelling — budgeting, forecasting and analysis — is an obvious area of use. Its varied and flexible screen and printer layout and, of course, its attractive graphic functions allow you to produce crisp, impressive presentations that can do so much to improve the image of a business. The preparation of invoices and estimates can be greatly simplified by integrating cost tables, calculations and printed output designs within a single sheet. Its data management facilities mean that it can be used as a database as well as a spreadsheet, and the vast body of data that could exist within a large spreadsheet can be sifted rapidly to find those few selective details that you need. There are very many other uses, both within the commercial world and elsewhere, for although SuperCalc has been developed mainly as a business management aid, it is equally applicable wherever you have numbers that need to be processed.

The focus of this book is on **using** SuperCalc3. The command set is explored and explained, but as far as possible this is within realistic applications that can be readily tailored to suit individual needs.

■ SECTION 2
Making your working copies

NEVER use your original disks as working disks. The only time they should come out of their case is when you are making copies. You will normally only need to do this once, when you first get the package, though it might be necessary later in the unlikely event of your working copies becoming unusable. Today's floppy disks are generally very reliable, but it is always possible to corrupt or erase files by mistake, and they can be damaged by careless handling.

SuperCalc3 is supplied with a program called STARTUP which is designed to produce working copies. The SuperCalc3 disk that will be created by STARTUP will be tailored to your printer and will be 'bootable', i.e. it will have the system tracks and the COMMAND.COM file that are used to start the PC off from cold. This has the obvious advantage of ease of operation. When you want to use the spreadsheet, all you will need to do is switch on your PC and slot SuperCalc3 – the copy of the PRODUCT disk – into drive A. It saves having to load up GEM or the MSDOS operating system first.

Copying the disks

1 Cover the write-protect notches on the original disks. This will prevent any accidental over-writing that can occur if you slot the wrong disk in the wrong drive. (It does happen!)

2 Boot up the PC with the MSDOS operating system (from Disk 1 of the Amstrad system disks), and leave that disk in drive A.

3 Prepare three new disks for your copies by formatting them. Use this command:

FORMAT B: /S   (Double drive machines)

FORMAT /S   (Single drive machines)

This will add the system tracks and the COMMAND.COM file to the disks.

4 Exit from FORMAT and replace the MSDOS disk with the SuperCalc3 disk PRODUCT. Type:

STARTUP

and follow the on-screen instructions.

5 Label your new copies, and store the originals and the backup copy of the PRODUCT disk in a safe place.

■ SECTION 2
Making your working copies

You should note that the versions created this way have no provision for using the mouse, and that several symbols will be different on the keyboard.

■   **SHIFT 2** produces @ (at) not '' (quotes).

■   **SHIFT** ' produces '' (quotes) not @ (at).

■   **SHIFT 3** produces # (hash) not £ (pound).

■   The £ key gives ' (apostrophe).

These are not major problems. The mouse software can be copied onto the SuperCalc3 disk (see Section 7), and you soon get used to the minor idiosyncrasies of the keyboard.

If you start the PC by using the standard GEM or MSDOS system, then run SuperCalc3, by typing SC3, these problems do not arise.

On the positive side, when SuperCalc3 is used directly from its disk, you will have more free memory than when it is run under the standard MSDOS operating system.

■ SECTION 3
The SuperCalc screen

When you enter SuperCalc3, you will meet the title screen:

```
                    SuperCalc3(tm)
                    Version  1.00
                      I B M   P C
                    S/N-002328 ,IBM DOS

                    Copyright 1983
                    SORCIM CORP.
                    San Jose, CA.




Enter "?" for HELP or "return" to start.
F1 = Help; F2 = Erase Line/Return to Spreadsheet; F9 = Plot; F10 = View
```

A couple of things to notice here. First, and purely for interest, note that SuperCalc is produced by the SORCIM Corporation — a most peculiar sounding name until you realize that it is MICROS backwards. At least their products are straightforward! Second, notice the line at the bottom of the screen:

Enter ''?'' for HELP or ''return'' to start:

''?'' (SHIFT /) will always take you to a help screen, wherever you are and whatever you are doing within SuperCalc3. There are a number of different screens, and the one you are shown will be related to the operation in hand at the time. These screens are useful reminders, though too compact to be of much use in explaining new concepts and functions.

Either the big L-shaped return key or the **Enter** key on the number pad can be used whenever SuperCalc3 asks for ''return'' (referred to hereinafter

11

■ SECTION 3
The SuperCalc screen

as RETURN). Press one and the screen will change to look like:

```
 !  A  !! B  !! C  !! D  !! E  !! F  !! G  !! H  !
 1|
 2|
 3|
 4|
 5|
 6|
 7|
 8|
 9|
10|
11|
12|
13|
14|
15|
16|
17|
18|
19|
20|
> A1
Width:  9  Memory:298 Last Col/Row:A1    ? for HELP
   1>
F1 = Help; F2 = Erase Line/Return to Spreadsheet; F9 = Plot; F10 = View
```

What you can see here is only part of the whole spreadsheet – the first 8 **columns**, A to H, and the first 20 **rows**. In fact the sheet has 63 columns, labelled A to Z, then AA to AZ and finally BA to BK; and 254 rows. You will see later how to move the sheet to bring other parts of it into view.

The column letters and row numbers are used to identify **cells**. Their coordinates are always given letter first, so that, for example, the top left cell is called **A1**. If you look at that cell now, you should see that it is highlighted by the **spreadsheet cursor**. Any data entered now will go into the cell A1.

At the bottom of the screen, below the 20th row, you will find a set of four lines:

■ **The STATUS line** tells you about the current cell – the one in which the spreadsheet cursor lies. When you first start it will show

>**A1**

The ''>'' at the start of the line shows the direction in which the spreadsheet cursor will move when you press RETURN.

The current cell is obviously A1, as you can see by glancing up at the main sheet, but you will appreciate this cell notice later when the cursor is in the middle of the screen and its exact position is less clear.

The other thing you will find on this line is a copy of anything that is written in the current cell.

■ **The PROMPT line** contains useful information. Most of the time it will be much as it is now:

Width: 9   Memory: 298   Last Col/Row: A1   ? for HELP

This tells you that the current column will display up to 9 characters – the visible width can be varied as you will see in Section 16; that you have 298 kilobytes of free memory available; that the bottom right-hand corner of the spreadsheet is at A1; and that you can get a HELP screen by pressing ''?''.

Later, when you start to use the SuperCalc commands, the PROMPT line will remind you of the options that are available within each command.

■ **The ENTRY line** is where data will appear as you first key it in. You will see a small cursor there:

1>_

The number at the beginning of the line tells you the position of the cursor within the entry line. At the moment it should show ''1'' as the cursor will be at the start. Type in something and watch the number change. We will return to this line shortly, in Section 6.

■ **The bottom line** reminds you that some of the function keys have special purposes.

F1 = Help;   F2 = Erase Line/Return to Spreadsheet;   F9 = Plot; F10 = View

We will look at these, and the other special keys in the next section.

■ SECTION 4
The SuperCalc keyboard

For the most part, the keyboard acts the same way under SuperCalc3 as it does normally, but there are some keys that should be noticed.

■ **F1** can be used instead of "?" to call up a Help screen at any time.

■ **F2** gives you a quick exit from the Data Entry line. If you have started to type a command but decided it was a mistake, F2 will get you out. If you are editing existing cell contents or writing something new, F2 will abandon it and leave the cell as it was.

■ **F9** will output the current Graph (if there is one) to your plotter or printer.

■ **F10** will display the current Graph on the screen.

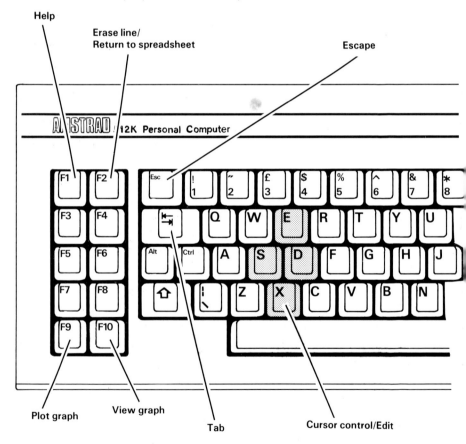

Help

Erase line/
Return to spreadsheet

Escape

Plot graph   View graph

Tab

Cursor control/Edit

■ SECTION 4
■ The SuperCalc keyboard

■ **Escape** has a very special purpose in SuperCalc3. If you press it, the reference for the current cell will appear in the Entry line. If you then move the spreadsheet cursor, this reference will change. The value of this key will become clearer later when we look at the Copy and Replicate commands in Section 12.

■ **Tab** is used in Editing to leap from/to the start or end of the line.

■ **E,S,D,X** if pressed with **Ctrl** can be used as an alternative to the normal arrow keys for cursor control and editing. If you choose to use the number pad for number entry, then these alternative cursor keys are worth remembering.

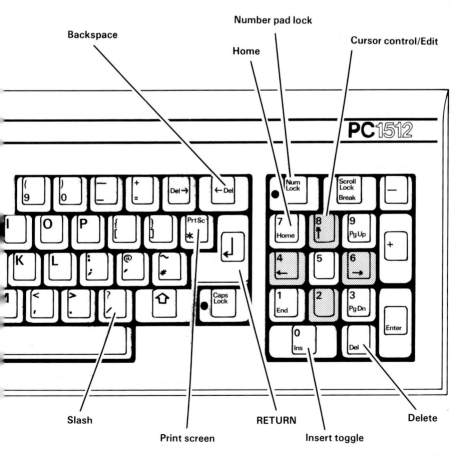

■ SECTION 4
The SuperCalc keyboard

■ **/** The Slash key gives you access to the SuperCalc3 commands. Type ''/'' and the Prompt line changes to:

Enter A,B,C,D,E,F,G,I,L,M,O,P,Q,R,S,T,U,V,W,Z,/,?

Pressing any of these keys now will call up the command that starts with the given letter. We will cover them all in time, but if you would like a quick browse, type ''/'' and a letter now. Remember that F2 will abandon a command and let you try something else. You might notice how the Prompt line changes for the different commands.

■ **?** will call up a Help screen. Should you ever want to include a question mark in any text written on the screen, then you must start the text with quotes to override the Help screen.

■ ***** Press **SHIFT *** to Print the Screen at any time.

■ **<DEL** does NOT delete. It will only backspace in the Entry line, and has no effect on the spreadsheet cursor.

■ The **RETURN** key has varying functions. Normally it is used – as you might expect – to signal that you have finished typing in some data, but when you are typing in a command line pressing RETURN has different effects, depending on where you are in the line. RETURN will also nudge the spreadsheet cursor along to the next cell.

■ **Num Lock** allows you to switch the number pad to numbers only. When the Num Lock light is on, you must press SHIFT to use the cursor control keys.

■ **Home** will make the spreadsheet cursor leap back to A1.

■ The **arrow** keys control the spreadsheet cursor and are also used in editing data in the Entry line.

■ **Ins** is a toggle switch – flipping between Insert and Overwrite modes for the Entry line. We will come back to this in Section 6.

■ **Del** will delete the character above the cursor in the Entry line.

■ SECTION 5
The spreadsheet cells

The contents of any cell will normally be of one of three types: either **text**, **numbers** or **formulae**. Strictly speaking, a number is a type of formula, but it is useful to keep the distinction between given numbers and calculated results. There are also some other less used types that we will come across later.

You do not have to specify what type your data is. SuperCalc3 will scan it as it is entered and decide its type. The most obvious effect of this is that if you mistype a formula, SuperCalc will treat it as a piece of text.

Let's explore cell contents and find our way around the screen by creating a very simple spreadsheet. It will take two numbers and perform some calculations on them.

It is possible that your sheet has acquired a scatter of items as you have been trying out things up to now. We can clear it by calling up the Zap command. Type:

/

Then press **Z**. The word **Zap** will appear in the Entry line, and the Zap options will show in the Prompt line. There are three: **Yes, No**, or **Contents**. Press **Y** to confirm that you want to Zap the Entire spreadsheet.

No is there in case you call up Zap by mistake. The **C**ontents option can be ignored for now.

After a Zap, the spreadsheet is completely clear and the cursor is back at A1. The title should go in here. We will call this one "SUMS". Type it in, on the Entry line — just the letters, no quotes are needed — then press RETURN. Notice that three things happen. The word appears in cell A1, the Entry line is cleared and the spreadsheet cursor moves on to the next cell to the right. Unless you turn the automatic movement off (see Section 11), the cursor will move in the direction shown in the Status line whenever RETURN is pressed. The direction will be that in which you were previously moving.

If you notice any errors while you are typing, press F2 and start again. If you see an error after the data has been transferred to its cell, go back to the cell and retype it. We will look at editing in the next Section.

Let's get out of B1 and build our spreadsheet elsewhere. Use the cursor keys to move the cursor back to A1 — notice how the contents of the cell appear in the status line — and then down to A3. Now type in:

Number 1

■ SECTION 5
The spreadsheet cells

When the data is entered, the cursor will carry on down to A4, where you can enter:

Number 2

After entry, the cursor will be in A5. Move it down another row, either by pressing RETURN or with the down-arrow key. Blank cells cost nothing in terms of memory use, and can improve the appearance of a sheet. With the spreadsheet cursor on A6, type in:

Add

Now move the cursor up and across to B3 and type in any number.Then take the cursor to the cell number.

Then take the cursor to the cell below – B4 – and enter a second number. We will get the spreadsheet to work out their sum. Move the cursor down to B6, next to the word ''Add'' and type in:

B3 + B4   (you can use small or capital letters)

Unlike text and numbers, the formula will not appear in the cell. What you will see instead is the result of the calculation.

Go back up to B3 or B4 and change the numbers. The new sum will appear almost instantly in B6.

Add two more active cells to the spreadsheet. At A7 type ''SUBTRACT'', then write ''B3 – B4'' into B7. Notice that if B4 contains a larger number than B3, the result will have a minus sign beside it, and appear in a different shade – **red** on a colour monitor.

You might like to add other cells to divide (B3/B4 or B4/B3) or multiply (B3*B4). You can use either the **PrtScr** key or **SHIFT 8** for the asterisk.

If a result doesn't look right, move the spreadsheet cursor to the relevant cell, and check the formula when it is displayed in the status line.

This is how your spreadsheet should look at this stage, though it has been set to display the formulae rather than the results:

The number calculated by a formula can be used in another formula. Move down to B10 and type in:

B6*2

This will double the sum of the two numbers given at the top. You might write ''ADD * 2'' in A10 to remind you what B10 does. Keep the

■ SECTION 5
The spreadsheet cells

```
   : A  :: B  :: C  :: D  :: E  :: F  :: G  :: H  :
 1│SUMS
 2│
 3│Number 1  9
 4│Number 2  5
 5│
 6│Add        B3+B4
 7│Subtract   B3-B4
 8│Multiply   B3*B4
 9│Divide     B3/B4
10│add * 2    B6*2
11│
12│
13│
14│
15│
16│
17│
18│
19│
20│
> B10            Form=B6*2
Width:  9  Memory:262 Last Col/Row:B10    ? for HELP
  1>
F1 = Help; F2 = Erase Line/Return to Spreadsheet; F9 = Plot; F10 = View
```

numbers simple in B3 and B4 and the effect of the formula will be obvious.

The formulae we have used here have all used simple arithmetic and have only involved two cell references. In practice, a lot of spreadsheet calculations are this simple — it is their combined effect that gives the spreadsheet its power; but other more complex operations can be performed. Most of the functions that are found on a standard pocket calculator are also available in SuperCalc3. The trigonometry functions — sines, cosines and the like — are there. You will also find logarithms exponentials and other mathematical functions, as well as statistical and logical operations.

■ SECTION 5
The spreadsheet cells

(You can, if you like, use SuperCalc3 as a calculator. Simply type the sum into the Entry line, and the result will appear in the cell. The numbers you are using do not have to be put into other cells first.)

There is also a range of functions that you will not find on a pocket calculator: ones that handle dates, some that perform compound financial calculations and others that analyse the contents of other cells in special ways.

SuperCalc3 sets no real limit to the complexity of the formulae that can be written, to the number of operations that are performed or cells that are referenced in the calculation. The only limitation is that the formula must not be more than 116 characters long! In practice, any formula that long would be far better broken down into several sections and worked out a bit at a time. Anything more than a dozen characters or so gets hard to understand.

■ SECTION 6
Editing in the Entry Line

So far, you will have corrected any typing errors by pressing F2 to clear the Entry line and starting again. Where you have typed only a few characters this is probably the best way to deal with errors. But if you need to change something in a longer expression — whether text, number or formula — it will be quicker to edit.

The cursor can be moved along the line by any of four keys. The left/right cursor keys (and **Ctrl S** and **Ctrl D**) may be used. **<-Del** will move the cursor back, though it will not delete.

Finally, there is the **Tab** key, below **Esc**. Pressing this will pull the cursor back to the beginning of the line, or make it leap to the far end if it is already at the beginning.

■   To **DELETE** a character, use **Del** on the number pad, or the cursor down key (or **Ctrl X**).

■   To **OVERWRITE** a character, move the cursor to it and type. This will work as long as you haven't toggled the Insert mode on.

■   To **INSERT** a character you have two options. You can open up a space in the line by pressing the cursor up arrow (or Ctrl E), which will shuffle the rest of the line to the right; new characters may then be typed into the space. Alternatively, press Ins to toggle the Insert mode. You will see the word INSERT appear at the bottom right of the screen.

Editing a cell

If you want to alter the contents of a cell, you can pull it back down to the Entry line with the Edit command. The simplest way to use it is to move the spreadsheet cursor to the relevant cell then press / and type **E** for Edit when the command prompt line appears. At the bottom of the screen, you will then see:

From? Enter cell
/Edit (into current cell)

Press RETURN to select the current cell. It will be copied into the Entry line where you can make your corrections. If you decide half-way through that you prefer the cell as it was originally, press F2 to abandon the Editing session.

It is also possible to copy the data from one cell into another by using the Edit command. Move the spreadsheet cursor to the cell into which you

Editing in the Entry Line

want to copy and call up Edit. When you are asked for the source cell, type its reference. The contents can be adjusted if need be before you press RETURN to transfer them to the new cell.

Where only a single cell is to be copied, Edit is often the simplest way to do it. But where a set of cells is concerned, the Copy and Replicate commands are usually more efficient.

■ SECTION 7
Of mice and GEM

The mouse

The mouse can be used instead of the cursor keys both for movement of the spreadsheet cursor and for editing in the Entry line. And it is not only movement. The left hand button duplicates the RETURN key, and the right hand one has the same effect as pressing "Escape".

If you are a mouse fan, you will, of course, want to use it, but even those less committed to mouse use may appreciate the extra speed when working on a larger spreadsheet. The cursor keys — like all the rest on the keyboard — have a built-in time lag before the auto-repeat takes over. This means that if you want to skim several cells in any direction it may be quicker to keep tapping the key rather than to hold it down and wait for the repeat. A mouse has no such time lag, so that you can whip around a large sheet or along a line that you are editing.

The corollary of this is that the mouse is very sensitive, and that it is quite easy to overshoot the target cell or to accidentally delete a large part of a line. A second point to bear in mind before installing the mouse, is that the software will take up a certain amount of memory and reduce the space available to the spreadsheet — from 298K to 293K. This is rarely likely to be a problem unless you have very ambitious plans!

If you do decide that you would like to have mouse control, there are two ways to go about it.

The simplest method is to run SuperCalc3 under GEM or the MS-DOS operating system that has been loaded in from a standard system disk. The mouse driver software is taken on board as the system starts, and will still be there for SuperCalc3.

If you prefer the convenience of running SuperCalc3 from its bootable disk, then the mouse software can be added to it. You need to copy the relevant file, then adjust the AUTOEXEC file so that it installs the mouse before running SuperCalc3.

1 Exit from SuperCalc3 by typing:

   /Q for Quit

   then **Y for Yes. You should now have the A> prompt.**

2 Check that you have at least 7000 bytes of space left on the disk by typing DIR. The free memory will be shown at the bottom of the list of files. If you are short of space, then delete the example spreadsheet files. They can always be read in from your backup copy if you need them. To delete them, type ERASE *.CAL

■ SECTION 7
Of mice and GEM

3 Insert Disk 1 of the operating system disks into drive A and your working copy of the SuperCalc3 disk into drive B. (On a single drive system, have Disk 1 in the drive and SuperCalc3 to hand.)

4 To copy the mouse software, type:

A> COPY MOUSE.COM B:

(Change disks when prompted on a single drive system.)

5 Now for the AUTOEXEC file. With Disk 1 still in drive A and SuperCalc3 in B, or to hand, call up the text editor:

A> RPED

6 Select the option, ''Edit an Existing File'', and give as the filename B:AUTOEXEC.BAT. When the file loads in, you will see that it consists of just two lines:

date
sc3

Take this opportunity to delete the DATE command. It serves no useful purpose on the Amstrad PC with its built in clock and calendar. Use the Del-> key to rub it out. Now type MOUSE in its place.

7 Exit from RPED, saving your new version of the file and check that the installation works. Put the SuperCalc3 disk in Drive A and reset the system by holding down, simultaneously, ALT, CTRL and DEL. You should see the message

Installing mouse driver

when the MOUSE command is met. Any error in your AUTOEXEC file will be obvious at this point, and can be corrected by going back over step 6. Try out the mouse and enjoy the speed with which it whips about the sheet.

GEM

The question here is whether or not it is worth running SuperCalc3 under GEM. The short answer is – No. There are no additional facilities available within SuperCalc3 under GEM, and it will run faster under MS-DOS. If you do prefer the ease and convenience of GEM for copying and deleting files, then it is always possible to do your disk management at another time when GEM is running.

PART TWO

Creating a spreadsheet

■ SECTION 8
The basic design

What you get out of a spreadsheet depends totally on what you put into it. A poorly planned sheet will give indifferent or even misleading results; and if the numbers that you feed into it are not accurate then the sheet may well compound those inaccuracies. On the other hand, with a good design and meaningful figures, a spreadsheet can be a valuable tool for forecasting, analysis and a lot more besides.

Over the next few sections we will create spreadsheet to handle a household budget. The design starts on paper – all the best spreadsheets begin life on the backs of old envelopes!

We will want to look at **Income** and **Expenditure**, and the difference between them, over a period of six months, working on a monthly basis. (Keep to six months rather than a year so that the sheet stays within the visible screen. Big sheets can wait till later.) The sheet can either be used to analyse past spending patterns – using carefully collected figures, or to budget for the future using estimates. A most effective way to use it is to include real figures for the first few months and to use these as the basis for projected spending.

We need to decide three things:

■   What figures are we going to put into the sheet?

■   What information do we want out of it?

■   How will we arrange our data in the rows and columns of the sheet?

For simplicity, we will assume that there is a single salary coming into the household. On the **Expenditure** side I have divided the outgoings into six categories: House, Food, Fuel, Clothes, Car and Miscellaneous. Before you go any further, check through your own expenditure pattern and see if these categories are appropriate. If they are not, now is the time to change them. The spreadsheet can be amended later, but is much easier to get it right from the start.

We want a number of results from the spreadsheet. On a monthly basis, we want to know the difference between Income and Expenditure. In the expectation that this will always be positive, we will optimistically refer to this as **Savings**. Over the period as a whole we also want to know the total spending in each category.

The data clearly needs to be arranged into a table, and we can do this in one of two ways. Either the figures for each month can be written across a row, with the category headings at the top of the screen:

■ SECTION 8
The basic design

```
:  A   ::  B   ::  C   ::  D   ::  E   ::  F   ::  G   ::  H   :
1:BUDGET
2:         Income  House  Food   Fuel   Clothes Car    Miscellan
3:
4:January
5:February
6:March
7:April
8:May
9:June
10:
11:Totals
```

or the data can be set out the opposite way, with a column for each month:

```
:  A   ::  B    ::   C    ::  D   ::  E   ::  F   ::  G   ::  H   :
1:BUDGET
2:         January February March  April  May    June   Totals
3:Income
4:
5:House
6:Food
7:Fuel
8:Clothes
9:Car
10:Miscellan
11:
12:TOTAL OUT
13:
14:Saving!
```

The latter arrangement is better. For a start, you have more headings than will fit across a single screen, and while your data can sprawl all over the sheet, it is always more convenient to keep it together as far as possible. Also, there is a convention in SuperCalc3 that time runs horizontally across the sheet. When you start to use the View command you will see that the x-axis of the graphs is assumed to be Time.

■ SECTION 8
The basic design

The first job to do on the spreadsheet is to write in its title and headings. If the title is written into cell A1, then it will be displayed, along with the filename, in the disk directory, as you will see later. Space the headings out to leave a gap of at least one row between the different parts of the sheet. For the moment, only fill in Column A, and the month in cell B2.

Type some figures for January's Income and Expenditure into cells B3 and B5 to B10, even though the formulae which will use them are not yet there. Use simple round figures that can be totalled manually. When you come to write the formulae you will find it useful to have a set of numbers in place so that the effect of the formulae can be checked as soon as they are written.

Did you notice that when you keyed in the data for cell B10, "Miscellaneous" in A10 was chopped down to "Miscellan"? As long as the cell to the right (B10) is empty, the text in A10 will be displayed in full. Once the next cell is in use, the number of characters that are visible will depend upon the width of the column. It can easily be changed using the Format command, as you will see in Section 15.

The first formula that is needed — in cell B12 — will total the Expenditure figures. You can get a total by simply adding together all the relevant cells; so B12 might read:

B5 + B6 + B7 + B8 + B9 + B10

There is a neater way to add a block of figures. It takes this form:

SUM(B5:B10)

SUM will work out the total value of the cells in the range that is defined in brackets. Note the colon that separates the reference for the start cell from that of the end cell. Check that the result you get is the one you would expect. If it isn't, then look carefully at your formula. Have you specified the correct set of cells in your SUM?

Two rows below, in B14, we need a formula to subtract this total from the Income given in cell B3. Type in

B3 − B12

Check the result, and if it isn't right, then make sure that you are referencing the correct cells.

28

■ SECTION 8
The basic design

When you are satisfied that the formulae work, replace the test figure in cells B3 to B10 with the most accurate ones you can get.

Did you manage to save anything in January?

You might like now to work your way across Row 2 and write in the month headings. But don't start to fill in all the data and formulae for those months yet, as there are some time-savers to be explored first.

■ SECTION 9
Copying cells

There are three SuperCalc3 commands that can be used where you need to write the same, or similar, data into two or more cells. You have already met **Edit**. The new ones are **Copy** and **Replicate**.

Edit is of most value in copying headings or other text from one individual cell to another. In the earlier example sheet we had two cells containing "Number 1" and "Number 2". It would have made sense here to Edit A3's contents into A4, changing the figure from "1" to "2" on the way.

You could use Edit to transfer a formula to a new cell. **SUM(B5:B10)** could be copied from B12 and edited to read **SUM(C5:C10)** before being entered into C12. It would be possible to do so, but quicker and more efficient to use either Copy or Replicate.Both of these commands have the ability to adjust cell references for you.

The COPY command

The best way to understand any command is to try it, so type

/C

for "Copy,". As with all commands, you only need give the initial. SuperCalc3 will write the rest of the word and the comma.

You will then be asked

From? Enter range or *graph-number

We will return to the idea of ranges shortly, and graphs can wait for a while. Right now we only want to copy the single cell, so type

B12,

Note that you can either type a comma after the cell reference, or press RETURN. If you do that, SuperCalc3 will supply the comma.

SuperCalc3 now needs to know to where it must copy the cell. You should notice here that the prompt line reads

To? (Enter cell); then <RETURN> or <,> for Options

Type:

C12

If you press RETURN at this point, SuperCalc3 will assume that you have finished giving instructions and get on with the job of copying. It will automatically adjust the cell references which were **B5:B10** in cell **B12**, to read **C5:C10** as it copies them into cell **C12**.

■ SECTION 9
Copying cells

If, for any reason, you do not want all cell references adjusted as a cell is copied — and there will be times when this is the case — then typing a comma after the destination cell reference will call up the Options, and show this prompt line:

N(o adjust), A(sk for adjust), V(alues), +, −, *, /

No adjust does precisely what you would expect. It leaves the cell references unchanged — useful if you wish to copy a particular formula from one part of the spreadsheet to another to make it easier to read or to include it in another calculation.

Ask for adjust can best be appreciated by trying it. The cell to be copied will be displayed in the entry line, and each cell reference in turn highlighted with the prompt:

Source Cell B12 Adjust *ref*? (Y or N)

This kind of selective adjustment is used where particular cells hold reference data that is to be used in calculations on a whole range of figures. You will see this in the Payroll spreadsheet in Section 18, where the tax rate in one cell is called up in the calculations for all of the employees.

Values copies only the numerical value of the cell — not the formula that produces it. The arithmetic symbols +, −, * and / are used when you want to combine the copied cell with the one into which you are copying. The addition option, for example, could be used to add a column of figures into a totals column.

You might like to explore one or more of these options in copying B14 into C14. Make sure that the final version reads **C3 − C12**!

The Copy command can be used with a block of cells, not just a single one. If yours is a well-regulated household, then the outgoings in each of the different categories should not change much from month to month. Let's copy all of the figures from B3 to B10 into the C column. Any odd differences can be corrected later. Type the following. The **bold** characters are those that you will key in. The others are those supplied by SuperCalc.

/Copy,**B3:B10,C3**

Note that the **From** range definition is given here, as in the SUM formula, by specifying the start and end cells with a colon in between. For the destination, you give the reference of the top left cell.

■ SECTION 9
Copying cells

We can fill in the next two columns, D and E, by using Copy on a larger scale. Watch the effect of this command:

/Copy,**B3:C14,D3**

In a similar way, you could copy any two columns from this area – perhaps B3:C14 again, or D3:E14 – to fill in the last two months of the year.

Work your way through the copied data to reflect any monthly variations in the figures, and you should be able to see any pattern that exists in your budget.

The next step is to work out our six-monthly totals and for that we will make use of the third of the cell-copying commands.

The REPLICATE command

At this stage, you should have a spreadsheet that looks something like this:

	A		B		C		D		E		F		G		H	
1	BUDGET															
2			January		February	March		April		May		June		Totals		
3	Income		800		800		800		800		800		800		4800	
4																
5	House		240		200		200		240		240		240			
6	Food		200		200		200		200		200		200			
7	Fuel		80		80		80		60		60		60			
8	Clothes		60		20		60		40		60		60			
9	Car		100		250		100		100		170		100			
10	Miscellan		100		60		90		120		100		100			
11																
12	TOTAL OUT		780		810		730		760		830		760			
13																
14	Saving!		20		-10		70		40		-30		40			

With a complete set of figures for the six-month period. The Income and Expenditure totals can now be written into column H. As we are totalling a solid block of figures, we can use the SUM function in the formula.

Into cell H3, type

SUM(B3:G3)

■ SECTION 9
Copying cells

(Depending upon the way that the spreadsheet cursor is moving when you press RETURN, the screen might shuffle sideways at this stage, bringing column I into view, and losing column A. Take the cursor over to column A (or press **Home**) to restore the main A to H display.)

Similar formulae are needed down the rest of the column, and for this kind of one-to-many copying you should use the Replicate command.

/**R**eplicate,

When you see the

From? (Enter range)

prompt, type **H3**. If the spreadsheet cursor is on that cell, then you can press RETURN instead. Where a cell reference is expected, pressing RETURN will write the current cell into the Entry line. For the **To** range, type **H5:H14**. Check that the command is correct, and use the normal editing keys if there are any typing errors. The Entry line should show

/ReplicateH3,H5:H14

As with the Copy command, Replicate will adjust all cell references automatically if you end the command with RETURN; or will offer No adjust, Ask for Adjust and Values options if you type a comma at this point. We want a full adjustment, so press RETURN.

You should now have a full set of totals in column H. Run the spreadsheet cursor down the list and check each cell's formula as it is displayed in the Status line at the bottom of the screen. Cells H11 and H13 will give zero totals as they are adding the contents of empty cells. They can be tidied out of the way by using the **BLANK** command. Where only the odd few cells are to be cleared, it is simplest to move the spreadsheet cursor to each in turn, type /**B** and press RETURN.

With the spreadsheet complete, you can now see where all the money is going, and perhaps arrange your finances a little better if they need it.

The Budget spreadsheet is very basic but will, I hope, have shown the essentials of spreadsheet construction as well as introducing the Copy and Replicate commands. You may like to save it and return to it later to tailor it to your own needs and to add to its facilities.

■ SECTION 10
Disks and files

Your spreadsheet files should be stored on a separate disk from the SuperCalc3 program files. This will prevent any accidental corruption of the program, but there is also the practical consideration that the working disk will not have a lot of free space on it.

On a double drive system it is simplest to reserve drive A for the program disk, and drive B for the spreadsheet files.

On a single drive system, replace the program disk in drive A with the spreadsheet file disk once SuperCalc3 is running. If you do use one of the rare commands that needs the program disk, then you will have to switch disks again for that.

When you start to develop and use proper working spreadsheets, you should get into the habit of making backup copies of your files on a second disk, so have one ready.

Saving a spreadsheet

Call up the Save command by typing

/**S**ave,

You will see the prompt

Enter Filename (or <RETURN> for directory)

Normally, you can simply type the filename at this point, but this time, press RETURN and have a look at the directory. The screen will display the SuperCalc3 Directory Options:

```
SuperCalc3 Directory Options
Program disk drive is C:
Current data disk drive is C:
Current spreadsheet file is : C:BUDGET3 .cal

OPTIONS:
     C(hange) data disk drive
     D(isplay) all files
     S(ee) .CAL spreadsheet files only
     E(nter) filename
     G(raphs) - current spreadsheet

F2 to abort command.
```

34

■ SECTION 10

Disks and files

Current drive and file information is given in the top set of lines. You should find that the current data drive is drive A. This will need changing to B on a double drive system, but before you do that, select the **D(isplay) all files** option to see the way that files are identified on a disk:

```
Directory of files on Disk:
AUTOBW   .bat  AUTOEXEC.bat  AVERAGES.cal  BALANCE .cal  BARCLAY .cal
BTUS     .cal  BUDGET1 .cal  BUDGET2 .cal  BUDGET3 .cal  BUDGET4 .cal
BUDGET5  .cal  BUDGET7 .cal  CASHONE .cal  CASHTWO .cal  COIN    .cal
CONSOL   .cal  COSTACC .cal  COSTTWO .cal  CUSTOMER.cal  DBASE   .cal
DRINKS   .cal  EOQ     .cal  FISHY   .cal  FONT    .dat  FORMATS .cal
HEAT1    .cal  HEAT2   .cal  HILO    .cal  JAN     .cal  LOOKUP  .cal
MORTONE  .cal  MOVING  .cal  OVERDRAW.cal  PAYROLL .cal  PETTY   .cal
PRESVAL  .cal  PRICING .cal  QUADGRAF.cal  QUADS   .cal  QUADS   .prn
RANGES   .cal  RANGES  .prn  REPLICA .cal  REPLICA .prn  S       .exe
SALES    .cal  SALES   .prn  SC3     .com  SC3     .hlp  SC3     .ovl
SC3BACK  .bat  SG1     .ovl  SG2     .ovl  SG3     .ovl  SG4     .ovl
SG5      .ovl  SG6     .ovl  SG7     .ovl  SG8     .ovl  SG9     .ovl
SIMULT   .cal  SIMULTA .prn  SIMULTB .prn  STANDEV .cal  STANDEVA.prn
STANDEVB.prn  STOCK   .cal  STOCK   .prn  STRLOAN .cal  STRLOAN .prn
SUMS     .cal  SUMS    .prn  SUMS2   .cal  SUMS2   .prn  TAX     .cal
TAX      .prn  TELPAD  .cal  TELPAD  .prn  VATRET  .cal  VATRET  .prn
QUADS    .sid  RANGES  .sid  REPLICA .sid  SALES   .sid  SIMULTA .sid
SIMULTB  .sid  STANDEVA.sid  STANDEVB.sid  STOCK   .sid  STRLOAN .sid
TAX      .sid  TELPAD  .sid  VATRET  .sid  COND    .com


<F2>=abort, <SP>=more...
  7>/Load,
Fi = Help; F2 = Erase Line/Return to Spreadsheet; F9 = Plot; F10 = View
```

35

■ SECTION 10
Disks and files

The Display option

You will see that there are two parts to each file's name. There is the **filename** itself. If you scan the directory, you will notice that the names, though brief, are fairly meaningful. **SC3** obviously refers to SuperCalc3; the **SG..** files are SuperCalc Graphics files; **AUTOEXEC.BAT** – the file that you may well have edited to install the mouse software – will AUTOmatically EXECute when the system is loaded.

Each filename is followed by a set of three letters separated by a dot. This is the **type extension** which describes the nature of the file. You should be able to find at least four different types of file on the SuperCalc3 disk.

■ **.COM** identifies a command or program file.

■ **.OVL** is an OVerLay file – part of a program that will be loaded into memory when it is needed.

■ **.HLP** is a HeLP file.

■ **.CAL** is a spreadsheet file.

You will not have to bother about giving type extensions with the names of your spreadsheet files. Just give the name and SuperCalc3 will add the .CAL on the end. Filenames must follow these rules:

■ Do not use more than eight characters.

■ Use only letters and numbers.

■ Do not include spaces in the name. If you need to split the name in two, use an underline. **BANK__AC** not **BANK AC**.

■ The name must mean something to you. Never use **SHEET1** or similar names. You will forget what they do within weeks, if not days.

The See option

This is the one that you will normally want to use as it selects out the .CAL files for display, and gives you more information than you will get from the simple Display option:

```
Directory of SuperCalc3 Files:
Filename      Version/Title
AVERAGES.CAL  SuperCalc ver.  1.00
AVERAGES
    Graph 1 -                                         Bar
         2 - SIMPLE HISTOGRAM                         Bar
BALANCE .CAL  SuperCalc ver.  1.00
BALANCES
BARCLAY .CAL  SuperCalc ver.  1.00
LOANS
    Graph 1 -                                         Line
BTUS    .CAL  SuperCalc ver.  1.00
B.T.U. Calculations
BUDGET1 .CAL  SuperCalc ver.  1.00
BUDGET
BUDGET2 .CAL  SuperCalc ver.  1.00
BUDGET
BUDGET3 .CAL  SuperCalc ver.  1.00
BUDGET
BUDGET4 .CAL  SuperCalc ver.  1.00
BUDGET
BUDGET5 .CAL  SuperCalc ver.  1.00
<F2>=abort, <C/R>=stop, <SP>=more...
    7>/Load,
F1 = Help; F2 = Erase Line/Return to Spreadsheet; F9 = Plot; F10 = View
```

For each spreadsheet file it shows the name, the date on which it was last used, and the contents of cell A1 — which is why that cell should be used for titles or other reminders about the sheet.

■ SECTION 10
Disks and files

The Change option

Return to the option page and press **C** to select the **C(hange) data disk drive** option. You will be prompted:

Drive to use

Press B if you have a double disk system. Leave it on A on a single drive system, and switch between program and data disks as needed.

Whichever drive you are using for your data disk, do make sure that there is a formatted disk in it at this point.

The **G(raphs)** option will be left until later.

Exit from the Options page by pressing **E** to select **E(nter) filename**.

You will be returned to the spreadsheet display, with the Entry line cursor poised to accept the filename. Type in ''BUDGET'' and press RETURN. The prompt line will now show:

A(ll), P(art) or V(alues)

All copies the entire spreadsheet onto the disk.

The other options are covered later in Section 25, File Management.

Select **A**ll now. The disk drive will whirr briefly, and your file will have been saved. You can check that it is there by going back into the Save command and pressing RETURN to get the Options. After you have checked the .CAL files, press F2 to abort the command and return to the spreadsheet.

When you come to save a spreadsheet for a second time and use the same name for it, then a new feature appears in the Save routine. After the filename has been typed, you will see this in the Prompt line:

Filename already exists. C(hange name), B(ackup) or O(verwrite)

Change name will simply let you try again with a new name.

Backup will take the existing file and give it a .BAK extension, then save the new sheet as the .CAL file.

Thus the existing BUDGET.CAL file would become BUDGET.BAK, and the new version of the sheet would be saved as BUDGET.CAL. If you wanted to load that original version again, you would have to give BUDGET.BAK as the filename.

Disks and files

Overwrite will save the new copy of the spreadsheet in place of the original one. Only select Overwrite if you definitely have no further use for the earlier version of the sheet. Otherwise, rename it or take the Backup option.

Loading a spreadsheet file from disk

The command here is /**Load** and the procedure is almost identical to that of Save.

Before loading a new spreadsheet, you should normally clear any existing one by using the Zap command. If you do not, the new one will merge with the old. Where the new sheet has something in a cell, it will overwrite the old; where cells are empty, the old sheet will show through. It can get really messy!

The exception to this is where both spreadsheets have an identical structure the new one will completely obliterate the old. There are also occasions where you will actively want to merge two sheets, as you will see later in Section 25.

After the command has been selected, by typing /L, you can either type in the filename immediately, or go to the options page to change drives or check the directory.

The Load options that you will be given are:

A(ll), P(art), C(onsolidate) or *graph-numbers

All will load in the whole file as it was saved. Stick with this simple option for now. We will return to the rest later when they can be put to use.

■ SECTION 11
The flexible spreadsheet

No matter how carefully you plan out a spreadsheet before you start, you may still find, once you have been using it for a time, that it needs extending or altering in some ways. There may have been things that you overlooked first time around, and circumstances do change. Fortunately, SuperCalc3 spreadsheets are not cast in concrete and adapting them is pretty straightforward.

You have already seen how to edit existing cell contents; and the Copy and Replicate commands that were met in Section 9 will clearly be of value when extending a sheet. But let us look first at three new commands that can be used for editing the whole spreadsheet. These are **Insert**, **Delete** and **Move**. We will also explore some of the Global command options in this Section.

Load in the BUDGET spreadsheet, if it is not already there, so that you have something to practice the commands on.

The GLOBAL command

In the default display mode it is the values produced by the formulae, not the formulae themselves, that are displayed on the screen. If you want to examine a formula, you have to take the spreadsheet cursor to its cell, so that the contents appear on the Status line.

Should you want to be able to keep an eye on all the formulae – as for example when altering the sheet – then you can make them appear using one of the **Global** command's options. Call it up with:

/Global,

The prompt line will show these options:

G(raphics),F(ormula),N(ext),B(order),T(ab),R(ow),C(ol),M(an)   or A(uto)?

Select **Formula**. This toggles the display of formulae on and off. When you have finished your alterations and want to make the values reappear, use the **/Global, Formula** sequence again.

The other option that you may like to note at this point is **Next**. This toggles the automatic movement of the spreadsheet cursor. When you are first building a sheet, and when you are entering quantities of data, it is useful to have the cursor move onto the next cell when you press RETURN. During an editing session, it may be worth suppressing this movement, as you may well want to remain in the same cell for a series of operations.

■ SECTION 11
The flexible spreadsheet

Use **/Global,Next** to stop the automatic movement, and again later to restart it.

The INSERT command

This command will let you insert new rows or columns into an existing spreadsheet. You can explore it with the BUDGET spreadsheet that was created earlier. I am assuming that the structure of your version is essentially the same as that shown here:

	A		B		C		D		E		F		G		H	
1	BUDGET															
2			January		February		March		April		May		June		Totals	
3	Income		800		800		800		800		800		800		SUM(B3:G3)	
4																
5	House		240		200		200		240		240		240		SUM(B5:G5)	
6	Food		200		200		200		200		200		200		SUM(B6:G6)	
7	Fuel		80		80		80		60		60		60		SUM(B7:G7)	
8	Clothes		60		20		60		40		60		60		SUM(B8:G8)	
9	Car		100		250		100		100		170		100		SUM(B9:G9)	
10	Miscellan		100		60		90		120		100		100		SUM(B10:G10)	
11																
12	TOTAL OUT		SUM(B5:B		SUM(C5:C		SUM(D5:D		SUM(E5:E		SUM(F5:F		SUM(G5:G		SUM(B12:G12)	
13																
14	Saving!		B3-B12		C3-C12		D3-D12		E3-E12		F3-F12		G3-G12		H3-H12	

We have omitted to include the heading 'Computers' in the Expenditure categories. Let's correct that, and slot in a new row between 'Car' − Row 9 − and 'Miscellaneous' − Row 10. The new row will then be Row 10, and the ones below that will all move down a row. Call up the Insert command:

/Insert

The prompt line will display only two options − **R(ow)** or **C(olumn)**. Select **Row**. SuperCalc3 will then ask for the **Row range**. As you only want to Insert a single row, type **10**. Only give the row number; Insert works right across the sheet, so column references are unnecessary.

You will see immediately that a space has opened up across Row 10, but look closer and you should see another change. All the formula in the bottom lines have been adjusted to fit the new spreadsheet arrangement.

The flexible spreadsheet

Where the total formula on Column B had read **SUM(B5:B10)**, it now reads **SUM(B5:B11)**. Similarly, the 'Savings' formula has been altered from **B3 – B12** to **B3 – B13**.

Where you Insert a row, or column, within an organised block, i.e. one that is defined in the range part of a formula, then the formula will be adjusted to cater for it.

The situation is rather different if you want to add onto a block, as we shall see shortly when we extend the sheet to handle a year's figures. But first, let's stay with the rows and Insert two at the top so that we can write in a second income, and calculate the total of these.

	A	B	C	D	E	F	G	H
1	BUDGET							
2		January	February	March	April	May	June	Totals
3	Income 1	800	800	800	800	800	800	SUM(B3:G3)
4	Income 2	200	200	200	200	200	200	SUM(B4:G4)
5	Total In	B3+B4	C3+C4	D3+D4	E3+E4	F3+F4	G3+G4	SUM(B5:G5)
6								
7	House	240	200	200	240	240	240	SUM(B7:G7)
8	Food	200	200	200	200	200	200	SUM(B8:G8)
9	Fuel	80	80	80	60	60	60	SUM(B9:G9)
10	Clothes	60	20	60	40	60	60	SUM(B10:G10)
11	Car	100	250	100	100	170	100	SUM(B11:G11)
12	Computer	50	50	50	50	50	0	SUM(B12:G12)
13	Miscellan	100	60	90	120	100	100	SUM(B13:G13)
14								
15	TOTAL OUT	SUM(B7:B	SUM(C7:C	SUM(D7:D	SUM(E7:E	SUM(F7:F	SUM(G7:G	SUM(B15:G15)
16								
17	Saving!	B5-B15	C5-C15	D5-D15	E5-E15	F5-F15	G5-G15	SUM(B17:G17)

There are two ways to go about this. You can Insert the new rows either above or below the current Income row. Both have their advantages and disadvantages.

If you Insert above, then you will have to Copy the Income data up from the new Row 5 to Row 3 before you can write the totalling formula in Row 5. On the other hand, by Inserting above, you have pushed Row 3 down to 5, and if the formula at the bottom will have been adjusted by the Insert command. **B3 – B13** will have been changed to **B5 – B15**.

■ SECTION 11
The flexible spreadsheet

If you Insert below, then the Income figures on Row 3 can be left as they are, but 'Savings' formulae will all need to be changed.

You will meet a similar problem if you extend the scope of the spreadsheet from six months to a year. At present, the months' figures – in Columns B to G – are totalled by formulae of the type **SUM(B3:G3)**; and we cannot Insert the July to December columns anywhere within this range without destroying the months' order! The new columns will have to go in columns H to M, and we will have to adjust the totalling formulae afterwards.

That sort of situation has no simple solution, but it could have been avoided by better planning at the start. We could have allowed for future expansion by leaving a blank column at either end of the range:

```
  :  A  ::  B  ::  C  ::  D \\  ::  H  ::  I  ::  J  ::  K  :
1 :BUDGET                    ))
2 :             JAN    FEB   ((  JUNE         TOTAL
3 :Income 1                  \\               SUM(B3:I3)
```

Here the SUM adds the columns from B to I, even though the months only use columns C to H. As empty cells have a value of zero, there is no harm in this. However, it does mean that you can Insert new columns between B and C, or between H and I, and the totalling formulae will adjust to accept them.

The DELETE command

For the most part, **Delete** is the equivalent of **Insert**. It can be used to remove whole rows or columns, either singly or in a set defined by a range.

As with Insert, you have to watch out for the effect on any formulae. If, for example, all the expenditure on House, Car, Computers and the rest made the Miscellaneous category unnecessary, then deleting that row (it should be Row 13 now), will cause a problem for the total formulae. They would read:

    SUM(B5:ERROR)

The **ERROR** tells you that the cell that had been referenced in that range does not exist. Try deleting that line, and see the ERRORs appear in the formulae; then switch the formula display off, and you will see that instead of numbers in the totals row you now have **ERROR**s (written in red on a colour monitor).

If you have called up the Delete command, you will have noticed that there is a third option in the Prompt line.

R(ow), C(olumn) or F(ile)

The **File** option allows you to delete spreadsheet files from the disk. Select it and you will be into the same kind of disk handling routines that you met earlier in Save and Load. You can either type in the filename directly, or press RETURN to access the disk directory options.

Delete files only if you need to. You can never be sure when you might need an old file, and there are no means of recovering a file once it has been deleted. SuperCalc3 files are fairly economical on disk space. None of the sample files that are described in this book will take up more than a few kilobytes, and even a fully fledged working file is unlikely to grow to more than 30 or 40K. There is room for a lot of files on a 360K disk, and disks are very cheap.

The MOVE command

Move can be regarded as a combination of Insert, Copy and Delete. It will take a range of rows or columns, open up a space for them elsewhere in the sheet, Copy them across, and then close up the place where they had been.

Like Insert and Delete, it can only be used on whole rows or columns. If you want to shift only part of a row, then you should use Copy, and Blank the cells where it had been before.

Any formulae referencing cells affected by the Move command will be adjusted, but you must watch out for ends of ranges.

On the BUDGET spreadsheet. it would be possible to Move the Income figure below the Expenditure ones — it might make it easier to use for some purposes. To do this would require the following command sequence:

/Move,Row,3:5,17

After this operation, the Expenditure rows will start at Row 4, and the Income figures will be in Rows 14,15 and 16. The spreadsheet will be unchanged from Row 17 downwards. Similarly, when moving columns, the one specified as the **To** column will be the first one to remain unchanged.

■ SECTION 12
Home with the range

The concept of ranges is crucial to many SuperCalc3 commands. A range may be:

■ **A cell**, defined by its column letter and row number – A3.

■ **A whole row**, defined by its number – 18.

■ **A whole column**, defined by its letter – F.

■ **A partial row**, defined by the start and end cells – B5:D5.

■ **A partial column**, defined by the start and end cells – A7:A14.

■ **A block**, defined by the cells in the opposite corners – normally top left and bottom right, though bottom left and top right may be used. Thus, C11:E16 and E11:C16 both apply to the same block.

■ **A set of rows**, defined by the top and bottom rows – 5:10.

■ **A set of columns**, defined by the left and right columns – B:G.

■ **The whole spreadsheet**, defined by the word **ALL**.

```
     !   A   !!   B   !!   C   !!   D   !!   E   !!   F   !
  1 !RANGES                                     Column
  2 !                                               F
  3 !Single cell  = A3                              :
  4 !                                               :
  5 !          Start.......Partial Row .......End   = B5:D5   :
  6 !                                               :
  7 !Start                                          :
  8 !   :                                           :
  9 !   :                                           :
 10 !Partial    = A7:A14                            :
 11 !Column              C11............................E11   :
 12 !   :                  :                         :   :
 13 !   :                  :        Block = C11:E16   !   :
 14 !End                   :        or E11:C16        :   :
 15 !                      :                         :   :
 16 !                    C16............................E16   :
 17 !                                               :
 18 !Row 18.................................................:......
 19 !                                               :
 20 !                                               :
```

45

■ SECTION 12
Home with the range

For the most part, the types of ranges that are possible with any given command will be self-evident, but if you do try to use an inappropriate range, SuperCalc3 will let you know. All commands are checked as they are entered, and any errors are reported back to you on the screen.

RETURN for the current cell

When you need to write a cell reference into a command, pressing RETURN will make the reference of the current cell — the one under the spreadsheet cursor — appear in the Entry line. It can save a little typing, but more importantly, it cuts down the chances of referring to the wrong cell.

Try it. Write something in a cell, then move the spreadsheet cursor back onto it and call up the Blank command. When it asks for the range, simply press RETURN.

   /Blank,<**RETURN**>

You can use RETURN in just the same way in those commands where a row number or column letter is required. To Insert a single row, for instance, you could move the spreadsheet cursor to the row where you want to open up a space and give the command sequence:

   /Insert,<**RETURN**>

ESCAPE to any cell

The **Esc**ape key serves a similar function to RETURN; press it when entering a command, and the current cell reference will be written into the command. There is, however, an important difference — when you press **Esc**, the cursor control is switched up to the spreadsheet cursor. Move it around and the cell reference in the Entry line will alter to suit. If you only want to get a single cell reference — perhaps as the point to which to Copy a block — then press RETURN when the cursor is on the right cell. If you need start and end cell references, press the colon (:) key when the start cell is reached. The next reference will then appear and can be adjusted with the cursor keys. Press RETURN or comma to finish the range entry.

The following example will show the way that you could use Replicate with RETURN and ESC to create a table of figures. Here it produces a simple multiplication table, but it could be a price list with varying discounts.

Home with the range

	A	B	C	D	E	F	G	H	I	J	K
1	REPLICATE										
2											
3		1	2	3	4	5	6	7	8	9	10
4	1	1	2	3	4	5	6	7	8	9	10
5	2	2	4	6	8	10	12	14	16	18	20
6	3	3	6	9	12	15	18	21	24	27	30
7	4	4	8	12	16	20	24	28	32	36	40
8	5	5	10	15	20	25	30	35	40	45	50
9	6	6	12	18	24	30	36	42	48	54	60
10	7	7	14	21	28	35	42	49	56	63	70
11	8	8	16	24	32	40	48	56	64	72	80
12	9	9	18	27	36	45	54	63	72	81	90
13	10	10	20	30	40	50	60	70	80	90	100

The table above was created by typing in only two figures and three formulae. All the rest of the cells were filled by the use of Replicate.

Start with the Row B3 to K3. Enter **1** in B3 and the formula **B3 + B3** in C3. Now, with the spreadsheet cursor on C3, call up the Replicate command, and press RETURN when asked for the **From?** range.

/Replicate,<**RETURN**>

SuperCalc3 is now waiting for the **To?** range. Press **Esc**. The Entry line should show this:

/Replicate,**C3,C3**

Use the cursor keys or mouse to move the spreadsheet cursor onto D3, the start of the range into which you are going to Replicate the formula. Note that the cell reference in the Entry line has changed. Press : to get to this:

/Replicate,**C3,D3:D3**

Move the spreadsheet cursor along to K3, and then – as you do not want the simple automatic formula adjustment – type a comma into the command. Select the **Ask for Adjust** option.

The formula **B3 + B3** will appear in the Entry line, and SuperCalc3 will highlight the first reference and ask if it should be adjusted. Type **Y** for that one, and **N** for the next. This will produce a row of cells reading:

	B		C		D		E		F		G	
3	1		B3+B3		C3+B3		D3+B3		E3+B3	.....		

In other words, the value produced in each cell will be 1 (the contents of B3) more than the previous cell.

Perform the same sequence of operations to fill the cells A4:A13 with the numbers 1 to 10:

```
       :   A   :
 1 :
 2 :
 3 :
 4 :   1
 5 :  A4+A4
 6 :  A5+A4
 7 :  A6+A4
 8 :.........
```

It is arguably quicker to type the numbers indirectly, when a simple 1..10 sequence is wanted, but this same technique can be used to produce any regular sequence of numbers. Also, all you need to do to change the range of numbers, is to alter the value in the starting cell. Put 10 there, and you will produce the sequence 10,20,30,...,100.

A single formula can be Replicated to fill in the body of the table. Move to B4, and enter **B3*A4**. Now Replicate this across the row C4:K4, using the RETURN and ESC keys, and the Ask for Adjust option. Adjust the first cell reference only, so that **B3*A4** becomes **C3*A4** and so on.

The whole row B4:K4 can be Replicated down to Row 13 with this command line:

   /Replicate,**B4:K4,B5:B13,A**sk for Adjust

Notice that the **To?** range specifies the column of cells that will be at the start of the Replicated rows.

The **A**sk for Adjust option will take a little longer to work through this time, as each cell reference in every cell from the source range will be presented in turn. You want it to adjust the second cell in each formula.

   B3*A4   C3*A4   D3*A4

will become:

   B3*A5   C3*A5   D3*A5

and so on down the rows.

PART THREE

Presentation on screen and paper

■ SECTION 13
The Format command

This is the key command for controlling the appearance of your spreadsheets. It is used for setting the widths of columns, the way in which numbers are displayed and position of text and values within cells.

Load in the BUDGET spreadsheet, and start to explore the potential of Format by improving the appearance of that sheet. Call up the command with **/F** and look at the Prompt line:

G(lobal), R(ow), C(olumn), E(ntry) or D(efine)

The first four of these are used to define the area of the spreadsheet to be set by the Format command.

■ **Global** refers to the whole spreadsheet.

■ **Column** and **Row** options must be followed by range references.

■ **Entry** allows you to pick out a single cell, partial row, column or block for special treatment.

■ The fifth option here is **Define**. This takes you through to the routines for defining your own display formats. We will return to this later.

After you have selected the range to be Formatted, the Prompt line will change to show the display options. As there are over a dozen of them, we will take them in several sets.

Column width

This can be set by giving the number of characters that you want to have visible. Remember that this does not alter the number that can actually be held in cells — the limit there is always 116 characters, or 16 digits in a value. You can only set widths for columns or the whole spreadsheet.

On the BUDGET spreadsheet, it might be an idea to expand column A so that 'Miscellaneous' can be shown in full. The columns holding figures are wider than they need to be; seven characters would be ample to hold values up to 999.99, and by squeezing the columns, you will be able to get one more on screen. Try these commands:

/Format,Column,A,13
/Format,Column,B:N,7

The Format command

Number display

The relevant options here are:

I(nteger),G(eneral),E(xponent),$,L(eft justify),R(ight justify)

You can try these out on the numbers in the BUDGET spreadsheet, or Save BUDGET, Zap the sheet clean, and set up a practice sheet as this:

```
   !   A    !!   B    !!    C    !!    D     !! E  !! F !!    G    !
 1 !NUMBERS
 2 !                                        Width 9  Width 6
 3 !General     Integer      Exponent    Money ($)  <---General--->
 4 !  .34567          0    3.4567e-1         .35  .34567  .35
 5 !    5.78          6    5.78e0           5.78    5.78  5.78
 6 !     42          42    4.2e1           42.00      42    42  Right
 7 !  123.45        123    1.2345e2       123.45  123.45 123.5  Justified
 8 !   1987        1987    1.987e3        1987.00   1987  1987
 9 !  1234567    1234567   1.234567e6   1234567.00 1234567 1.2e6
10 ! 15000000000 15000000000  1.5e10    >>>>>>>>>>  1.5e10  2e10
11 !
12 !.34567        0         3.4567e-1    .35        .34567  .3457
13 !5.78          6         5.78e0       5.78       5.78    5.78
14 !42           42         4.2e1        42.00      42      42
15 !123.45      123         1.2345e2     123.45     123.45  123.5  Left
16 !1987       1987         1.987e3      1987.00    1987    1987   Justified
17 !1234567   1234567       1.234567e6   1234567.00 1234567 1.2e6
18 !15000000000 15000000000 1.5e10       >>>>>>>>>> 1.5e10  2e10
```

Note: If the spreadsheet has been set to display formulae, by a **/Global,Formula** command, then these Format options will not alter the screen display. Values will continue to be displayed in the default mode. As the key sequence **/G,F** can be very easily typed in error for **/F,G**, you should check for Formula display if the Format options do not seem to be working.

Key a varied set of numbers into the cells A4 to A10; Copy or Replicate them, first down to A11:A16, then across the rows B:F − or beyond if you want to add other combinations of display formats of your own. Use the following series of commands to impose different formats onto the

■ SECTION 13
The Format command

columns, and you will be able to see the effects of those formats:

/Format,Global,**12**

This is by no means necessary, but the larger cells do allow bigger numbers to be displayed easier.

Column A will need no Format command, as the **General** format is the default mode. In this format, numbers will be displayed as they best fit — which means as they are typed, or in Exponent format if they are too large (see below).

/Format,Column,**B,**Integer

Any numbers with decimal fractions will be rounded to the nearest whole number. This is for display purposes only. The number is held with full accuracy in the spreadsheet's memory.

/Format,Column,**C,**Exponent

In **exponential** or scientific notation, the numbers are divided into 'digits' and powers of ten. The 'digit' part will always be a value between 1 and 10, i.e. the decimal point is after the first figure. Multiply this by the power of ten given after the **e** to get the true value of the number. Thus:

1.234e2

means 1.234×10^2, or 1.234×100 or 123.4. Likewise

3.456e − 1

means 3.456×10^{-1} or $3.456 \times 1/10$, or 0.3456.

/Format,Column,**D,**$

This displays all numbers with two digits after the decimal point as it is essentially a money format — dollars and cents, or pounds and pence. Use this format Globally on the BUDGET spreadsheet.

/Format,Column,**E,9**
/Format,Column,**F,6**

The last two columns have been given reduced widths so that you can see how the **General** format alters the display to suit the space available. You will notice that large numbers are converted to exponential form, and and that decimal fractions are rounded to fit. If columns are very narrow, the readings can well be misleading: 15000000000 (15 billion) is written as 1.5e10 in the 9 character column (E), but in the tight space of column F it is written as 2e10 — a difference of 5 billion from its real value!

If there is insufficient space for a long number in an **Integer** or $ format cell, the number display will be replaced by >>>>>>>.

Justification

L(eft justify), R(ight justify)

The second aspect to the number display is the position of the numbers within the cells. Normally the numbers will be justified to the right, i.e. the digits will end on the right-hand side of the cell. Where the numbers have the $ format — this means that the pounds and pence are neatly arranged in columns.

/Format,Column,B:E,$,Right

would give a neat monetary display in columns B to E. The **Right** option would only need to be specified where Left justification had been previously specified.

Left justification can be selected where you want to pull a column of figures closer to the column to the left for ease of reading.

Text justification

T(ext) L(eft justify),T(ext) R(ight justify)

This is controlled by separate options, so that the same area could be set to justify numbers and text to opposite sides. For example:

/Format,Global,Left,TextRight

Special formats

H(ide) will make the contents of a cell invisible. The main uses of this option are to keep confidential information away from prying eyes, and also to tidy up complex spreadsheets by removing any intermediate calculations from view.

■ SECTION 11
The flexible spreadsheet

* will produce an asterisk display, converting numeric values into strings of asterisks, e.g.

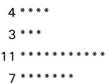

This is a left-over from earlier versions of SuperCalc, and has little utility in the current version with its full graphic abilities.

Default restores the standard settings – General, numbers, Right and Text Left justified, with a column width of 9.

User-defined formats – selected from the range 1 to 8. These are all the same until reset on the option screen called up by the /Format,Define option, and will display numbers as money values, with a dollar sign at the left and commas used as separators, e.g.

123456 would appear as **$123,456.00**

The Format command should be used regularly in the spreadsheets created from now on, as a clearly laid out screen does much to make a spreadsheet easier to use – and therefore more effective.

■ SECTION 14
Price setting

This section shows how SuperCalc3 could be used to set the price of a new product by calculating the profitability at different prices and estimated sales levels. It is similar to the BRKEVN sample spreadsheet given with SuperCalc3 and is a good example because it demonstrates a number of things very well. It shows that:

■ You can do very useful work with very simple formulae — it is their combined effect that counts.

■ SuperCalc3 allows you to test out a whole range of possibilities in the time that it would take to work through the figures once with a pocket calculator.

■ The design and layout of the spreadsheet are important, not just from the point of view of ease of use, but also in how they affect the way that the sheet is used.

The task

We want to know what price to set for a new product. The spreadsheet cannot give us the answer to this directly, but it can tell us what level of sales we would have to achieve to secure profitability at different price levels.

The working data

We know the costs that are involved in the production of our new line — a 'Home Budget' software package — and can break them down into *Fixed* and *Variable* costs. This data will form the basis of the spreadsheet's calculations.

The marketing staff have a reasonable idea of the kind of sales that can be expected at different retail prices. The figures are written onto the sheet for reference, though not used actively in calculations. That could be done, but would be far more complicated. Also, these figures are only *estimates*. If you use them to produce a final result, there is a danger that you might treat it as an accurate figure! SuperCalc3 will happily produce results that are *inaccurate* to 16 decimal places, if the data that it uses is inaccurate.

The spreadsheet design

We want to be able to see three sets of information — the basic data on prices and costs; the profits over a range of sales levels; and the marketing estimates. They can be conveniently arranged in three pairs of columns:

	A		B		C		D		E		F	
1	PRICE & PROFITS											
2					SALES LEVEL		PROFIT/LOSS		EST.SALES		@ PRICE	
3	PRODUCT		HomeBudget		500		(B19)*C3-B1		50000		10	
4	RETAIL PRICE		19.99		C3+C3		(B19)*C4-B1		20000		F3+5	
5	DISCOUNT		40		C4+C3		(B19)*C5-B1		5000		F4+5	
6	WHOLESALE PRICE		B4-B5%B4		C5+C3		(B19)*C6-B1		3000		F5+5	
7					C6+C3		(B19)*C7-B1		1500		F6+5	
8	FIXED COSTS				C7+C3		(B19)*C8-B1		1000		F7+5	
9	Development		10000		C8+C3		(B19)*C9-B1		500		F8+5	
10	Marketing		4000		C9+C3		(B19)*C10-B		250		F9+5	
11	Other		2000		C10+C3		(B19)*C11-B		100		F10+5	
12	TOTAL		SUM(B9:B11)		C11+C3		(B19)*C12-B		50		F11+5	
13					C12+C3		(B19)*C13-B12					
14	VARIABLE COSTS		(Per Unit)		C13+C3		(B19)*C14-B12					
15	Labour		2.25		C14+C3		(B19)*C15-B12					
16	Material		4		C15+C3		(B19)*C16-B12					
17	Packaging		2.50		C16+C3		(B19)*C17-B12					
18	TOTAL UNIT COST		SUM(B15:B17)		C17+C3		(B19)*C18-B12					
19	UNIT PROFIT		B6-B18		C18+C3		(B19)*C19-B12					

Prices and Costs   Column A is used for headings, and should be set to at least 12 characters wide to avoid the use of clumsy abbreviations. Column B is for the Price and Cost figures and formulae.

The **Retail price** is the basis of our sales estimates, and the figure that we will change most often when the spreadsheet is used. As the **Discount** is a known percentage, this can be used to calculate the **Wholesale Price**. The formula is:

Retail price − Discount % of retail price

This translates to the SuperCalc3 formula in B6:

B4 − B5 % B4

Price setting

The % sign calculates the percentage. It is equivalent to dividing by 100 before multiplying. Here, you could get the same result with **B4 − (B5/100)*B4.**

Fixed costs have been divided into **Development, marketing** and **Other.** In practice, the marketing costs in particular may vary for different sales levels, but they will be treated here as fixed. Any variations could be keyed in as the spreadsheet is being used. The **Total** can be produced by a SUM formula.

Variable costs are here based on unit costs, and ignore any possibility of mass-production savings.

The **Unit profit** is calculated from the **Total unit cost** and the **Wholesale price.**

Key in the headings, formulae and figures for prices and costs, as they are given in the figure above, and in the same cells. If you do run a business in which this kind of price setting exercise is appropriate, then once the spreadsheet has been completed and you have seen how it works, you may want to tailor it to suit you.

Sales Level and Profit   We do not know at the outset whether we should be examining sales in the range 100 to 1000, or 10,000 to 100,000. Rather than write in a fixed range of numbers, therefore, we will construct one that can be easily changed. The technique is the same as that seen earlier in the multiplication table. Look at column C in the figure above:

```
        |  D  |
     3|  500
     4|  C3+C3
     5|  C4+C3
     6|  C5+C3
```

By altering the value in C3, the whole range can be changed.

The **Profit/loss** figure is calculated by subtracting the Fixed costs from the Gross profit (Unit profit * Sales). The formula should be written into D3 in the form:

  B19*C3 − B12

Replicate this down column D, using **Ask for adjust** so that only the C reference is changed.

■ SECTION 14
Price setting

Estimated sales at varying prices These may be written onto the spreadsheet in columns E and F for ready reference. Use the **/Global,Formula** command to toggle on the display of formulae and check yours against the figure above. When you have made any necessary corrections, use the command again so that the sheet displays values.

Before you use the spreadsheet:

■ Call up the **/Global,Next** command to toggle off the automatic cursor movement. For much of the time that the spreadsheet is in use, you will want to keep the cursor in cell B4, where the possible retail prices will be entered.

■ Select the **/Global,Column** command to alter the **Order of Recalculation**. Normally, SuperCalc3 works through a spreadsheet by calculating each row, left to right, before moving down to the next. This order is not appropriate to the layout used here, as the **Unit profit** must be found before the **Profit/loss** figures can be calculated. This means that a value from the bottom of column B is needed for work at the top of column D. Switching to column-based recalculation will achieve this. The **/Global,Row** command will restore row-based calculation.

Putting the Pricing spreadsheet to work

From the marketing staff's estimates, it would appear that mass sales could be achieved if the 'Home Budget' can be produced cheaply enough. A glance at the total variable costs will show that there is no possibility of reaching a retail price of £10:

Try entering '14.99' as the retail price. Column D shows losses at all sales levels — but the range is only from 500 to 8500. Change the figure in C3 to 5000, so that the range goes up to 85000 sales. You will see that a break-even point is reached — but only at 65000 +, far higher than the marketing staff have predicted.

Change the retail price to 19.99, and Column D will switch to solid profits. The range in Column C needs to be altered again — put 500 in C3. You can now see that sales of 5000 — which are said to be likely — would just bring in a profit.

Increase the retail price to 24.99, and the break-even point drops down to around 2500. This is comfortably below the predicted sales at this price, and if 50% more sales could be achieved, the project would show a healthy profit of over £12000.

Trying higher retail prices will show that even though the break-even point drops steadily, the predicted sales fall even faster. The price is clearly going to have to be around £24.99.

■ SECTION 15
Printouts

There are two ways in which you can get printouts from SuperCalc3. The quick, but crude, way is to use the **Prt Sc** key. Press **SHIFT** and **Prt Sc** and the Amstrad PC will dump a copy of the screen onto the printer. It is a complete copy — Status, Prompt and Entry lines and all — but it may well be sufficient for many working purposes.

If you want a tidier and more controlled printed result, then you should use the **Output** command. Call it up with /**O**utput, and you will be presented with this Prompt line:

   D(isplay) or C(ontents)

In essence, **Display** is the sheet as you see it, while **Contents** is a list of the cell numbers and the numbers, formula or text written into them. A Contents output would normally be selected only where you wanted to check the formulae in a spreadsheet that perhaps wasn't working quite as well as it should.

Select **D**isplay. You will now be asked for the **range**. This should be given as the references for the top left and bottom right cells of the block that you want to print. It can be smaller than the visible screen area, or larger — though you should be aware of the limitations of your printer. We will return to that later. For the moment, assuming that you are working with the Pricing spreadsheet, a range of **A1:F20** will cover the whole working area.

The Prompt line now moves on to the next level of options:

   P(rinter), S(etup), C(onsole) or D(isk)

Make sure your printer is turned on, press **P** and you will have a hard copy of your sheet.

Improved printouts

■ *Turn off the Border* — the display of column letters and row numbers. This must be done before you start to use the **Output** command, by using the /**Global,Border** option. Use it again later to toggle the display back on. Note that when the Border is removed, it will be more difficult to work out the cell references for the range. Make a note of them first.

■ *Use Format to the full.* It may be worth changing column widths so that information can be seen more easily, and the **Hide** option can conceal any working calculations that are not actually needed in your printed version. Justify text and numbers so that they line up well.

■ SECTION 15
Printouts

■ Check the final appearance on screen before sending to the printer. You can do this by selecting **Console**, i.e. the monitor, at the last level of the Output options. It is quicker than printing, and saves paper.

■ Use the **Setup** option to customise the output to your printer. The command sequence:

/Output,Display,*range*,Setup,...

brings you to the choice of Setup options:

L(ength), W(idth), S(etup), A(uto FF), D(ouble space), or P(rint)

Length is the number of lines and may be anything from 0 to 255. The default value is 66.

Width may be anything up to 255 characters per line. The default setting of 132 is for extra wide paper, or for a compressed typeface on A4 paper.

Auto Form Feed is a toggle switch – normally off, so that SuperCalc3 waits for a space bar press at the end of each page.

Double Space is also a toggle switch, and normally off.

Setup allows you to send control characters to the printer – usually to select a new typeface. The control characters are those specified in your printer manual. Suppose that you wanted to use a compressed type so that a wide block could be squeezed onto a page. The printer manual might tell you to send the sequence After you have selected the **Setup** option, press the **Esc** key then **SHIFT-C**. Nothing will appear on the screen, which can be disconcerting, but the characters will have been output to the printer. The new typeface – or any other printer setting will then be used for that print run, and for all subsequent printing until the machine is reset, or **Setup** is used again.

Print will start the printer.

An Output command that sets the printer to 70 lines in bold typeface (where ESC B selects bold) and then prints the block from A1 to F18, might therefore look like this:

/Output,Display,**A1:F18**,Setup,Length70, Setup,<**ESC**><**SHIFT-B**>, Print

■ SECTION 16
Payroll calculations

The Payroll spreadsheet that will be developed in this section will show how SuperCalc3 can be used to produce payslips, as well as calculating the payroll. It also introduces the use of that most valuable function — **IF**.

The task

To calculate and print out the wage slips for six employees, on the basis of the number of hours worked that week. The wage slips are to show Gross pay, Tax and Net pay.

The working data

The names, normal working hours, basic rate of pay and tax thresholds of the employees are as given below. All overtime is paid at time and a half.

Employee	Basic hours	Basic rate	Tax-free limit
Bloggs, F.	35.0	£4.00	£60.00
Brown, W.	35.0	£5.00	£90.00
Entwhistle, A.	35.0	£6.00	£60.00
Jones, B.	35.0	£6.00	£60.00
Robinson, E.G.	40.0	£3.00	£40.00
Smith, A.E.	40.0	£5.00	£60.00

Tax is to be calculated at 30% on the first £250 of taxable income per week, and 40% on any income above that. No employee earns enough to qualify for tax at the higher rates, which can therefore be ignored.

(The spreadsheet has been deliberately simplified so that its structure and the techniques involved are clearly visible. Any real payrolling spreadsheet would have to include National Insurance, pensions and other additions and deductions, as well as maintaining a running total of all weekly figures.)

The calculations

These fall into three sets: Hours, Pay and Tax. If we can work out the formulae for the first employee, F.Bloggs, they can be replicated to all the others. As data for each employee will be in a single column, with the calculations working down from the Hours worked at the top to Net pay at the bottom, the spreadsheet must be set to recalculate by columns. Use the command **/Global,Column** to select this.

Hours   The Hours worked must be compared with the Basic hours to find the Overtime hours, if any.

■ SECTION 16
Payroll calculations

Hours worked is to be entered weekly into cell B4. Basic hours is written permanently into cell B5. Overtime will be calculated into B6. In English, the Overtime formula can be expressed as:

If Hours worked is more than Basic hours, then Overtime is Hours worked minus Basic; otherwise, Overtime is nil.

SuperCalc3 has an **IF** function that can be used in formula in this way:

IF(test, value-if-true, value-if-false)

In other words, IF the expression that is tested is found to be true, then the first value will be written into the cell; if it is false, the second value will be used.

For the Overtime calculation, it yields this formula:

IF(B4>B5,B4-B5,0)

where B4 is Hours worked, and B5 is Basic hours. Compare this formula with the English version given above and see how they both say the same thing.

Pay   This set of formula and data is held in Rows 9 to 13 in the following manner:

```
 !     A     !!    B    !!          C            !
 8!Hourly Rate    4           5
 9!Overtime Rate  B8*1.5      C8*1.5
10!Basic Week     IF(B4>B5,B5 IF(C4>C5,C5*C8,C4*C8)
11!Overtime Pay   B6*B9       C6*C9
12!GROSS          B10+B11     C10+C11
```

The Basic hourly rate is written permanently into the spreadsheet. The Overtime rate is time and a half on the Basic.

The Basic pay cannot simply be calculated by multiplying Basic hours and Basic rate, as this would not allow for those weeks where the Hours worked fell below the required minimum − and this job is hourly paid! It must be worked out by this formula:

If the Hours worked are more than Basic hours, then multiply the Basic hours by the Basic pay; if not then multiply the Hours worked by the Basic pay.

Payroll calculations

We can translate it into SuperCalc3 in stages. First, write it in formula style, but using recognisable terms:

    IF(Worked>Basic,Basic*Basic rate,Worked*Basic rate)

Then replace the terms with cell references for the first column:

    IF(B4>B5,B5*B8,B4*B8)

The **Overtime pay** calculations present no problems. Multiply the Overtime hours by the Rate — if there has been no Overtime, then the zero in that cell will produce a zero value here.

Gross pay is a simple addition.

Tax calculations:

```
   |    A      ||        B         |
14 |Tax Free      60
15 |Taxable       B12-B14
16 |Tax @ rate 1  IF(B15>0,B22%B15,0)
17 |Tax @ rate 2  IF(B15>B23,B24%(B15-B23)
18 |Total Tax     B16+B17
19 |
20 |NET PAY       B12-B18
21 |
22 |TAX RATE 1    30
23 |TOP LIMIT     250
24 |TAX RATE 2    10
```

Tax free (B16) is a permanent value, representing the amount that can be earned each week before tax becomes payable. This is deducted from the Gross pay (B13 − B16) to get the **Taxable** amount.

There are at least two different ways of working out how much tax is payable. The first way would look like this, if calculated on paper:

	Amount	Rate		Tax
Taxable pay	290			
Tax band 1	250	@ 30%	=	75
Tax band 2	40	@ 40%	=	16
Total tax				91

■ SECTION 16
Payroll calculations

The tax payable at standard rate is then calculated in two stages. First find the taxable amount — which will be the maximum for the band (here £250), or the whole taxable amount if this is less than the maximum. The formula would be (in English):

IF(Taxable>Maximum1,Maximum1,Taxable)

The amount taxable at Rate 2 would then be found in the same way that Overtime hours were calculated:

IF(Taxable>Maximum1,Maximum1-Taxable,0)

This will then give you the amount over the Tax band 1 maximum, or a zero value.

The tax payable at each rate can then be found by multiplying the taxable amount by the percentage rate.

This method is perfectly satisfactory, and can be extended fairly readily to cater for tax at higher rates. However, a different method is used in this spreadsheet, if only to demonstrate that there is always an alternative. It also produces the same results in fewer formulae.

On the Payroll spreadsheet, *all* taxable pay is taxed at the standard rate, then any taxable pay above the Band 1 maximum is taxed again at 10% — the difference between Rate 1 and Rate 2.

Taxable pay	290	@ 30%	=	87
Above Band 1	40	@ 10%	=	4
Total tax				91

As you can see, the result is the same either way.

The formulae are worked out through these steps:

Tax @ Rate 1 = IF(Taxable>0,Rate 1% of Taxable, 0)

Tax @ Rate 2 = IF(Taxable>Maximum,Rate 2% of Taxable — Maximum,0)

which gives in B18 and B19:

B18 = IF(B17>0, B22 % B18, 0)
B19 = IF(B17>B23, B24 % (B17-B23), 0)

■ SECTION 16
Payroll calculations

Completing the spreadsheet

If the Tax rates and Limit in cells B22 to B24 are replicated across the spreadsheet, then the formulae that use them can also be replicated with the simpler automatic adjustment. If you wish to save a little space, you can hold that tax data in B22:B24 only and replicate the formulae using the **Ask for Adjust** option. Either way, it makes no difference to the results.

For ease of reading, it will be worthwhile to Format column A to a width of at least 14, and the other columns to 10 or 12. This will allow headings and names to be displayed in full, though it will mean that column G disappears off the right of the screen. We will see in the next section how to cope with large spreadsheets.

Protect your work. The only data that would need to be regularly altered on this kind of spreadsheet are the **Hours worked** entries. All the rest of the cells should be rewritten rarely, if ever. It is a good idea, therefore, to protect those cells against accidental alterations. We can do this with the **Protect** command.

The simplest way to manage it is with this sequence:

> /Protect,**ALL**

This turns protection on for the entire spreadsheet. Now release the row in which Hours worked is written:

> /Unprotect,**B4:G4**

The most visible effect of the **Protect** command is to change the colour, or tone, of the writing in those cells — but more importantly, it is not possible to enter data into them.

If you do need to alter wage rates or tax data, then the relevant cells can be **Unprotect**ed at will.

Producing the wage slips

If you look at the full printout of the Payroll spreadsheet you will see that the **Gross pay, Tax** and **Net pay** figures for each employee are copied from the main table down to separate lines below. Any other information that is needed on the payslips — works number, department reference or whatever — could be written in as text.

Printing the wage slips is then a simple matter of using the **Output** command to send each employees block of cells to the printer in turn.

■ SECTION 16
Payroll calculations

	A		B		C		D		E		F	
1	PAYROLL											
2			Bloggs, F		Brown, W.	Entwhistle,A		Jones, B.		Robinson,E.		
3	HOURS											
4	Worked		40.00		30.00		55.00		35.00		40.00	
5	Basic		35.00		35.00		35.00		35.00		40.00	
6	Overtime		5.00		.00		20.00		.00		.00	
7	PAY											
8	Hourly Rate		4.00		5.00		6.00		6.00		3.00	
9	Overtime Rate		6.00		7.50		9.00		9.00		4.50	
10	Basic Week		140.00		150.00		210.00		210.00		120.00	
11	Overtime Pay		30.00		.00		180.00		.00		.00	
12	GROSS		170.00		150.00		390.00		210.00		120.00	
13	TAX											
14	Tax Free		60.00		40.00		60.00		60.00		40.00	
15	Taxable		110.00		110.00		330.00		150.00		80.00	
16	Tax @ rate 1		33.00		33.00		99.00		45.00		24.00	
17	Tax @ rate 2		.00		.00		8.00		.00		.00	
18	Total Tax		33.00		33.00		107.00		45.00		24.00	
19												
20	NET PAY		137.00		117.00		283.00		165.00		96.00	
21												
22	TAX RATE 1		30.00									
23	TOP LIMIT		250.00per Week									
24	TAX RATE 2		10.00									
25												
26												
27			Gross Pay		Tax		Net Pay					
28	Bloggs, F		170.00		33.00		137.00					
29												
30												
31			Gross Pay		Tax		Net Pay					
32	Brown, W.		150.00		33.00		117.00					
33												
34												
35			Gross Pay		Tax		Net Pay					
36	Entwhistle, A.		390.00		107.00		283.00					
37												

■ SECTION 17
Titles and windows

As spreadsheets grow larger, it becomes increasingly difficult to keep track of what each column and row is doing. With the Payroll spreadsheet, for example, the headings on Column A will disappear off the side of the screen when you start to use those columns to the right of F. It is possible to cram more columns into a screen by reducing their widths – but this is rarely an attractive solution. Far better to use either Titles or Windows.

Titles

The **Title** command allows you to lock the left-hand column(s) and/or the top row(s) of the spreadsheet. Then, when the spreadsheet is scrolled, the Title area remains static, while the rest scrolls beneath it.

The **Title** command shows four options in its Prompt line:

H(oriz)., V(ert)., B(oth) or C(lear)

The **Horizontal** version of the command will lock the current row and all above it.

You might like to try it on the Payroll sheet. Move the spreadsheet cursor to a cell in row 2 – where the names are, then type:

/Title,Horizontal

Now move the cursor down the sheet and press on beyond row 20. You will see that the rows from 3 onwards scroll up under the locked Title rows (see overleaf).

The **Vertical** option works in much the same way. It locks the column containing the spreadsheet cursor, and all others to its left. Place the cursor in column A of Payroll and type /Title,Vertical to lock the headings. Now, no matter how far your sheet extends to the right, by scrolling the screen, any employees figures can be brought near to the headings column.

Both gives you Horizontal and Vertical Title areas. It does not lock the whole top corner solid, but instead holds the side headings when scrolling left-right, and the top headings when moving up-down.

Using any new **Title** command will undo the previous one, or use the **Clear** option to remove all title locks.

■ SECTION 17

Titles and windows

:	A	::	B	::	C	::	D	::	E	::	F	:
1	PAYROLL											
2			Bloggs, F		Brown, W.		Entwhistle,A		Jones, B.		Robinson,E.	
13	TAX											
14	Tax Free		60.00		40.00		60.00		60.00		40.00	
15	Taxable		110.00		110.00		330.00		150.00		80.00	
16	Tax @ rate 1		33.00		33.00		99.00		45.00		24.00	
17	Tax @ rate 2		.00		.00		8.00		.00		.00	
18	Total Tax		33.00		33.00		107.00		45.00		24.00	
19												
20	NET PAY		137.00		117.00		283.00		165.00		96.00	
21												
22	TAX RATE 1		30.00									
23	TOP LIMIT		250.00per		Week							
24	TAX RATE 2		10.00									
25												
26												
27			Gross Pay		Tax		Net Pay					
28	Bloggs, F		170.00		33.00		137.00					
29												
30												

```
> F24
Width: 12  Memory:258 Last Col/Row:L36    ? for HELP
   1>
F1 = Help; F2 = Erase Line/Return to Spreadsheet; F9 = Plot; F10 = View
```

Note: When a Title area has been locked off, you cannot move into it with the spreadsheet cursor. You must either leap into it with the **Home** key, or use the = (Go to) facility. To get into a Title area, or to leap to a new part of the spreadsheet (on any occasion), press the equals key (=). You will see this in the Entry line:

   = >(Enter cell)

Give the reference for the cell to which you want to move.

If the destination cell is on the visible screen, then the spreadsheet cursor will simply move there. If it is not currently visible, then the spreadsheet will be redisplayed to bring it into view.

Titles and windows

Windows

The Title command is intended mainly for keeping headings visible alongside widely spread entries. It could also be used more generally to lock one part of the sheet while pulling a more distant part into view, so that two sets of data may be compared. A better command for this purpose, however, is **Window**.

Window will allow you to split the screen, either vertically or horizontally, at any point. The two halves can then be scrolled independently in any direction, or synchronised to scroll together. The windows can be treated as separate screens, in that each can have its own Title locks, and any **Global** command will only work in the window in which it was given.

This makes it possible to have one window set to display values, and the other to show formulae. The same cells can then be viewed at the same time in both modes — useful for checking your formulae.

The spreadsheet cursor can be moved from one window to the other by pressing the semi-colon key (;).

The options for this command are:

   H(orizontal), V(ertical), S(ynchronise), U(nsynchronise) or C(lear)

In the **Horizontal** split, the bottom half, including the current row drops down one row to make room for a second display of row numbers. If the **Synchronise** option is also selected — within the same command or afterwards — then scrolling either window left or right will drag the other window along with it. Vertical scrolling will only affect the current window.

With a **Vertical** split, the right side of the spreadsheet moves right to allow a second vertical border. If the windows are Synchronised, then any vertical scroll will be in both halves simultaneously.

Unsynchronise will free the connection between the two halves; and **Clear** will restore the single screen display.

Note: it is not possible to Output a split window display to the printer, but you can get a screen dump using the **Prt Scr** key.

■ SECTION 18
Note and coin analysis

If you are working out the payroll with SuperCalc3, then you ought to be working out the pay packets with it as well. The Note and Coin Analysis that will be developed in this section could be written directly onto the existing Payroll spreadsheet. Alternatively, develop it as a separate sheet as it is done here, and merge the two together later.

The task

To find out what combinations of notes and coins are needed to make up the pay packets for the employees, and to calculate the total value and total number of each denomination.

The calculations

These will be based on *integer division*, as we are only interested in whole notes and coins. For instance, if you wanted to pay the sum of £75 in cash, it is of little help to know that it will take 3.75 £20 notes. You want to be told that it takes 3 £20 notes and that there is £15 remaining.

In SuperCalc3, we can find the whole number by using the **INT** function. This gives the Integer of a number, i.e. its whole part only, ignoring any decimal fraction. Thus:

INT(75/20)

gives the answer 3.

There is a second function that can be used to find the remainder from an integer division. That function is **MOD**:

MOD(75/20)

gives the answer 15, as 70 divided by 20 is 3, with a remainder of 15.

These two functions can be used together to work through the various denominations, from the top down. We could carry on with our present example to find what other notes were needed to pay the bill.

INT(15/10)
MOD(15/10)

These will tell us that we need one £10 note, and that there is £5 remaining.

Note and coin analysis

The spreadsheet design

We will design the spreadsheet so that each employee's pay packet is analysed across a row. We will therefore need columns for three note denominations (£20, £10, £5) and six coins (£1, 50p, 20p, 10p, 5p, 1p) — but that will take 16 not 9 columns, as we need to know the whole number and the remainder at every denomination until the last.

The sheet will therefore be rather wide and very cluttered, as half the data on it will be made up of intermediate calculations — the remainders. These are important to the spreadsheet, but irrelevant to the user. When all the formulae have been written in and checked, we will tidy up the appearance by some selective Formatting, to finish up with a spreadsheet like this:

	A	B	D	F	H	J	L	N	P	Q	R	S
1	COIN & NOTE ANALYSIS											
2			Notes				Coins				UNIT	NUMBER
3	Pay	#20	#10	#5	#1	50p	20p	10p	5p	1p	#20	48
4	136.79	6	1	1	1	1	1	0	1	4	#10	4
5	168.95	8	0	1	3	1	2	0	1	0	#5	4
6	253.90	12	1	0	3	1	2	0	0	0	#1	16
7	109.84	5	0	1	4	1	1	1	0	4	50p	5
8	153.50	7	1	0	3	1	0	0	0	0	20p	7
9	217.34	10	1	1	2	0	1	1	0	4	10p	2
10											1p	2
11	TOTAL	48	4	4	16	5	7	2	2	12		
12	Values	960	40	20	16	2.5	1.4	.2	.1	.12		
13												
14	Total Pay											
15	1040.32											
16	Total Notes											
17	1020.00											
18	Total Coins											
19	20.32											
20	CHECK TOTALS	OK										

Headings   Assuming that the layout shown above is used, the note and coin denominations should be entered into ALTERNATE cells in row 3, starting B3, D3, F3..., etc. The intermediate columns must be left clear for remainder calculations.

Note and coin analysis

The first row is

```
   !    A   !!    B    !!    C    !!    D    !!    E    !
 3 |Pay        20            10
 4 |(any value) INT(A4/20) MOD(A4,20) INT(C4/10) MOD(C4,10)
```

Do put a value in A4, and make it an irregular one, like '136.79' as this will test out the formulae as they are entered. Note that each pair of formulae work on the same value. Those in B4 and C4 both use the **Pay** in A4; D4 and E4 work on the remainder in C4.

These first four should give results like this:

```
   !    A   !!    B    !!    C    !!    D    !!    E    !
 3 |Pay        20            10
 4 |  136.79      6      16.79      1        6.79
```

It is possible to use the Copy command to fill in the next few columns, but it may well be simpler to type them in directly.

```
   !    F   !!    G    !!    H    !!    I    !
 3 | 5
 4 | INT(E4/5) MOD(E4,5) INT(G4) (G4-H4)*100
```

Notice the different formula where the units change from pounds to pence. G4 − the remainder after £5s have been removed − will show **1.79**. The INT value of this is 1 − the £1 coins. The pennies remaining are then multiplied by 100 to convert them to integers so that the formulae may continue for the coins.

```
   !    J   !!    K    !!    L    !!    M    !!    N    !
 3 | 50p         20p           10p
 4 | INT(I4/50) MOD(I4,50) INT(K4/20) MOD(K4,20) INT(M4/10)
```

```
   !    O   !!    P    !!    Q    !
 3 |           5p            1p
 4 | MOD(M4,10) INT(O4/5) MOD(O4,5)
```

If your formulae are all entered correctly, then row 4 should show the following figures:

```
Pay     20   10   5    1    50p  20p  10p  5p   1p
136.79   6    1   1    1     1    1    1    0    1    4
```

Replicate the formulae down for as many rows as you need; leave a blank row for future expansion; and then add totalling formulae at the bottom to find out how many notes and coins of each denomination are needed. On

■ SECTION 18
Note and coin analysis

the sample spreadsheet, the totals are in row 11, and have the form **SUM(B4:B10)**

The core of the spreadsheet is now complete. What remains are those features that may help to make it easier to use.

For a start, it might be an idea to Insert a new column at A, so that employees' names, or reference numbers, can be written into the sheet − this will not be necessary if it is planned to merge this sheet with the earlier Payroll spreadsheet.

We can improve the readability of the analysis by copying all the final totals across to produce a neat list:

UNIT	NUMBER
£20	B11
£10	D11
£5	F11

....

We can check the accuracy of the analysis by comparing the total of the original Pay figures with the total value of the Notes and Coins.

On the sample sheet, the value at each denomination is worked out beneath its total. Thus B11 shows how many £20 notes, and B12 shows the value of them. Pay, Notes and Coins are totalled separately − the figures may be useful at the bank:

```
 !          A          !
14|Total Pay
15|  SUM(A4:A10)
16|Total Notes
17|  B12+D12+F12
18|Total Coins
19|  H12+J12+L12+N12+P12+Q12
```

The spreadsheet does its own check with the formula:

  IF(A17 + A19 = A15,"OK","NO")

Notice that in this expression, the messages "OK" or "NO" will appear in the cell to show the result of the check. We have previously only assigned number values within IF formulae, but text values may be assigned: "Text Values" must be enclosed in quotes and must not exceed 9 characters.

■ SECTION 18
Note and coin analysis

Formatting the display

If you have followed the construction of this spreadsheet as it has been given, you will now have one that sprawls across more than two screen widths, and is therefore difficult to use. Let's improve the display.

The remainder figures, in columns C, E, G, ..., etc., are not needed on screen. They could be concealed by the /**Format**,...,**Hide** option, but it will be more effective here to shrink the column widths. This will tuck the remainders out of sight and close up the spreadsheet at the same time. Work across the relevant columns with commands like this:

/Format,Column,C,1

(The width can be set to 0, so that the columns disappear altogether, but this has the disadvantage that the cursor also disappears if it is in one of them!)

The display should be much clearer after this, though still too wide for the screen. None of the cells in the Notes and Coins columns should contain more than three or four characters, so they too could be shrunk — a width of 5 should be sufficient. At that size, the entire working sheet is visible. As the same formats will be used when the spreadsheet is printed, you should now be able to get a print out of your Note and Coin analysis ready for making up the pay packets.

Note and coin analysis

Linking to Payroll

1 Make a note of the Last Col/Row figure in the Status line of the Analysis spreadsheet. If you followed the layout of the illustration above it will be S20. This will be needed later. Then save the sheet under the filename 'Notes'.

/Save,NOTES,All

2 Clear the current spreadsheet.

/Zap,Yes

3 Load in the PAYROLL file:

/Load,PAYROLL,All

4 Find a clear area to the right of, or beneath, the Payroll working space. Note the reference of the top left cell of this area − on my version of Payroll, J1 marks the start of free space. This is where the Notes sheet will fit when it is merged. Load in that file using the Part option. To do this you must specify the range of the spreadsheet that is to be merged. As you want all of it, give the references of the top left cell and of the Last Col/Row noted at Step 1.

/Load,Notes,Part,A1:S20,J1

5 Replace the written figures for Pay in the first column of the Notes part with the references of the relevant Net pay cells in the Payroll part.

If you have used the layout shown in these sections, then the references B12, C12, D12, ..., will be needed in column J between J4 and J9.

6 Note that when using the spreadsheet, you should force an additional recalculation (press !) after the last Hours worked figure has been entered. The Payroll calculations all work down the columns, while those in Notes are performed across the rows. A final recalculation will ensure that all values are updated.

PART FOUR

The working spreadsheet

■ SECTION 19
Functional formulae

As a general rule, if you can express any relationship as a mathematical equation, then you can convert it to a SuperCalc3 formula. Sometimes it will take a series of formulae, rather than just one; but there is almost always a way to get the maths onto the spreadsheet.

Conversions

If you have the basic ratios needed to convert figures from one form to another — Metric to Imperial, Dollars to Pounds, Centigrade to Fahrenheit, or whatever — then you can work them into formulae within spreadsheets, or use SuperCalc3 to produce conversion tables for reference.

Temperature may be the simplest place to start because you have only a single unit on either side — degrees F and degrees C. The conversion equations are:

$$C = (F - 32) * 5/9$$

and

$$F = (C * 9/5) + 32$$

Both can be transferred very easily to the spreadsheet, by substituting cell references for the letters in the equations.

```
    !    A   !!  B   !!  C   !
  1 |CONVERT TO CENTIGRADE
  2 |Degrees F   Degrees C
  3 | (value)    (A3-32)*5/9
```

Here you would be expected to write the Fahrenheit figure in A3. It could be expanded into a ready reference table by writing a range of values in column A, and replicating the formula down column B.

Length, weight and volume conversions present slightly more complex problems, as in each form of measurement several units are used — yards, feet and inches into metres and centimetres; gallons, pints and fluid ounces into litres and millilitres.

The best solution is probably to reduce the mixed measurements to the smallest units; convert that figure, then divide again later. So you would change yards, feet and inches into inches, change those to centimetres, then express them in larger units if need be.

■ SECTION 19
Functional formulae

```
|  A   !!  B   !!  C   !!       D       !!  E   !
1|LENGTH - GOING METRIC
2|Yards?  Feet?   Inches?  = Inches      = Cms.
3|(value) (value) (value)  A3*36+B3*12+C3 D3*2.54
```

To convert a measure in centimetres into Imperial units, we can divide by the same basic ratio (1 inch = 2.54 cm), then use integer division to get the higher units.

```
|  A   !!  B   !!   C    !!       D       !!    E    !
1|LENGTH - THE EMPIRE STRIKES BACK
2|Cms.?   = Inches = Yards     Feet          Inches
3|(value)  A3/2.54  INT(B3/36)  INT(B3/12)-C3*3  MOD(B3,12)
```

The cell to look closely at there is D3. The formula is:

INT(B3/12)-C3*3

INT(B3/12) will give the number of whole feet in the B3 inches, but you must take from this those feet that have been 'used up' by the yards. An alternative approach would be to use an intermediate calculation to find the number of inches left over after the yards have been taken — MOD(B3,36) — then divide that value by 12 to get the feet result.

Other metric conversions should follow the same pattern. These basic ratios may be of use:

LENGTH	1 mile = 1.61 kilometres
	1 km = 0.621 mile
WEIGHT	1 ounce = 28.3 grammes
	1 gramme = 0.0353 oz
AREA	1 square inch = 6.45 square centimetres
	1 acre = 0.405 hectare
	1 ha = 2.47 acres
VOLUME	1 cubic inch = 16.4 cubic centimetres
	1 fluid ounce = 28.4 millilitres
	1 litre = 0.22 gall
FUEL USE	1 mpg = 2.82 km litre

Functional formulae

The VAT fraction

Finding a percentage of a given value is simple enough, if you know the percentage and the base figure; but working backwards is not so simple — as anyone who has to handle VAT knows only too well.

Adding VAT to a total is easy:

```
    :   A   ::   B   ::   C   :
10|             Total     (value)
11|Vat at       15        B11%C10
12|             Inc. Vat  C10+C11
```

The VAT figure could be used directly in the formula in C11, instead of putting it into a cell and calling it up from there. However, this method does make it much easier to amend the spreadsheet should the VAT rate change in the next budget.

Finding how much of a VAT inclusive bill is composed of VAT is another matter. HM Customs and Excise advise you to use the **VAT fraction** — currently 3/23:

```
    :   A   ::   B   ::   C   :
10|             Total     (value)
11|             VAT       C10*3/23
12|             Ex. Vat   C10-C11
```

The 3/23 VAT fraction is produced by simplifying the fraction 15/115, i.e. the VAT percentage over 100 + the VAT percentage. We are better off using the full expression in our spreadsheets. Then, when the VAT rate changes, the new rate can be written in without having to calculate a new — and possibly more complex — fraction:

```
    :   A   ::   B   ::         C          :
10|             Total     (value)
11|Vat at       15        C10*B11/(100+B11)
12|             Ex. Vat   C10-C11
```

Functional formulae

Income tax

While we are on the subject of tribute to HM Government, let's look again at Income Tax. It has been tackled in the Payroll spreadsheet, but for weekly wages, and not over the full range of tax bands.

The sheet that is shown here will take an annual income, and find the amount of tax payable in each band. Look closely at the formulae in columns C and E. These calculate the amount of taxable income in each band, and the remainder to be taxed at higher rates.

C8 has the formula IF(C5>A8,A8,C5) which translates to:

IF TAXABLE is more than MAXIMUM-1, use MAXIMUM-1, otherwise use TAXABLE

D8 finds the remainder, if any, with IF(C8 = C5,0,C5-C8) This means:

IF AMOUNT-TAXED equals TAXABLE, no remainder, otherwise deduct AMOUNT-TAXED from TAXABLE

The same formulae are used, with minor variations, throughout the bands.

	A	B	C	D	E	F
1	TAX CALCULATION					
2						
3	Annual Income		25000			
4	Tax Allowance		3155			
5	Taxable Income		C3-C4			
6						
7	Threshold	Rate	In band inc.		Tax	Remainder
8	14600	30	IF(C5>A8,A8,C5)		B8%C8	IF(C8=C5,0,C5-C8)
9	2600	40	IF(E8>A9,A9,E8)		B9%C9	IF(C9=E8,0,E8-C9)
10	4090	45	IF(E9>A10,A10,E9)		B10%C10	IF(C10=E9,0,E9-C10)
11	5000	50	IF(E10>A11,A11,E10)		B11%C11	IF(C11=E10,0,E10-C11)
12	Top band	60	E11		B12%C12	
13						
14			Total Tax		SUM(D8:D12)	

■ SECTION 20
Job costing

In this section we will look at using SuperCalc3 for job costing, taking as our example a central heating firm that needs to produce estimates for installation work.

The task

To find the cost of materials and labour for an installation, and to give a guide for the price that is to be charged. You will notice that two different prices are in fact produced by this spreadsheet.

The **Minimum job price** is the amount required to cover the cost of the job – but without giving any profit. Doing the job at this rate will at least cover the workers' wages, so may be worth considering when business is poor.

The **Preferred Estimate** includes a contribution to the fixed overheads of the firm, as well as the target profit margin. This is the price the firm will hope to get.

The sheet would not be used for producing customers' estimates – not in its present form. Those sensitive calculations at the bottom are not for outside eyes, and the layout is not likely to impress the discerning potential customer. We will look later at ways of drawing the required information out in a presentable form.

The spreadsheet design

The basic sheet is shown opposite. To keep things simple, only a small selection of radiators and other parts have been included in the list, and **Labour** costs are entered as global figures at the end.

On a full working version, this columnar layout could lead to a very long spreadsheet, but it is the logical layout for easy use by the estimator, and will print out well. If the user does need to keep an eye on the total costs while working in the **Materials** section, then the sheet can be split by the **Window** command. This would bring the bottom lines into view.

No problems arise here with the calculations. The cost of each type of item is found by multiplying the unit cost (in column C) by the number required (entered into column D). Totals, and the percentages for Overheads and profit are all simple formulae.

Setting up the spreadsheet could be fairly time-consuming, depending upon the number of different items that have to be included in the list, but

```
    !  A  !!  B  !!  C  !!  D  !!  E  !!  F  !
  1 !CENTRAL  HEATING  ESTIMATES
  2 !
  3 !FOR
  4 !
  5 !MATERIALS              PRICE   NUMBER    COST
  6 !BOILER    43000 BTU  220                D6*C6
  7 !          53000 BTU  250                D7*C7
  8 !          65000 BTU  300                D8*C8
  9 !CYLINDER             45                 D9*C9
 10 !CISTERNS 10 LTR   3                     D10*C10
 11 !          40 LTR   8.5                   D11*C11
 12 !          70 LTR   11.5                  D12*C12
 13 !CONTROL UNIT       70                   D13*C13
 14 !PUMP               27.5                 D14*C14
 15 !RADIATOR SING.600  16                   D15*C15
 16 !          SING 1200 19                   D16*C16
 17 !          SING 1800 33                   D17*C17
 18 !          DOUB 800  33                   D18*C18
 19 !          DOUB 1200 60                   D19*C19
 20 !          DOUB 1600 69                   D20*C20
 21 !THERMO VALVES      5                    D21*C21
 22 !TUBE     15mm      .95                  D22*C22
 23 !          22m      1.75                 D23*C23
 24 !                                        D24*C24
 25 !LABOUR   Skilled   6                    D25*C25
 26 !          Unskilled 4.                   D26*C26
 27 !
 28 !Total costs        .................. SUM(E6:E26)
 29 !Variable Overheads @10%    ......... 10%E28
 30 !Minimum job price          ......... E28+E29
 31 !Contribution to Fixed Overheads @5% 5%E28
 32 !Target Profit Margin @ 15%          15%(E30+E31)
 33 !         PREFERRED ESTIMATE........ SUM(E30:E32)
```

■ SECTION 20
Job costing

you do have the consolation of knowing that it will only need doing the once — apart from updating the prices from time to time.

When the spreadsheet has been finished and tested, it should be cleared of all test data — the figures in column D — by the /**Blank** command. The empty sheet can then be saved on a new, blank disk. This empty file will be loaded in whenever a new job is to be costed, but at the end of each costing exercise, the finished sheet should be saved under the customer's name or reference. With around 360K per disk, but only 3 or 4K per spreadsheet, you will be able to store almost a hundred copies on a single disk.

Improvements and adaptations

In many businesses it is possible to cost the Labour required to install each item in the Materials list. The spreadsheet could be extended to include this.

The Labour should be written in on the basis of the time per unit of each item, with separate columns for each category of skilled and unskilled worker:

	C		D		E		F		G	
4							SKILLED	TIME 1		
5	PRICE		NUMBER		COST		PER UNIT	THIS ITEM		
6	220		1		C6*D6		4.5	F6*D6		
...										
...										
15	16		4		C15*D15		1.5	F15*D15		
16	19		5		C16*D16		1.75	F16*D16		

Where a job involves a number of different trades, the spreadsheet could grow quite large, and setting it up will be slow. But the benefits will be apparent as soon as it is put to use. The estimator will only need to enter the number of each of the items that are needed, and all the rest of the work will be done by the spreadsheet. There should be a very significant amount of time saved on hunting through price lists and job-time reference tables. As a fair proportion of estimates never result in actual work, the less time spent on them the better. (Though I hope that the accuracy and thoroughness of your spreadsheeted estimates will help you to secure a far higher proportion of acceptances!)

```
     |  A  ::  B  ::  C  ::  D  ::  E  ::  F  |
 1:CENTRAL  HEATING  ESTIMATES
 2:
 3:FOR       Mr. I.C.Cauld
 4:
 5:MATERIALS              PRICE   NUMBER    COST
 6:BOILER   43000 BTU    220.00       1   220.00
 7:         53000 BTU    250.00             .00
 8:         65000 BTU    300.00             .00
 9:CYLINDER               45.00       1    45.00
10:CISTERNS 10 LTR         3.00       1     3.00
11:         40 LTR         8.50             .00
12:         70 LTR        11.50             .00
13:CONTROL UNIT           70.00       1    70.00
14:PUMP                   27.50       1    27.50
15:RADIATOR SING.600      16.00       1    16.00
16:         SING 1200     19.00       2    38.00
17:         SING 1800     33.00       1    33.00
18:         DOUB 800      33.00       2    66.00
19:         DOUB 1200     60.00       1    60.00
20:         DOUB 1600     69.00             .00
21:THERMO VALVES           5.00       7    35.00
22:TUBE    15mm            .95              .00
23:        22m            1.75      60   105.00
24:                                         .00
25:LABOUR   Skilled        6.00      24   144.00
26:         Unskilled      4.00      24    96.00
27:
28:Total costs       ................   958.50
29:Variable Overheads @10%   .........    95.85
30:Minimum job price         .........  1054.35
31:Contribution to Fixed Overheads @5%    47.93
32:Target Profit Margin @ 15%            165.34
33:        PREFERRED ESTIMATE........    1267.62
```

■ SECTION 20
Job costing

Customers' estimates

The customer will want only a selection of the information that is contained in this spreadsheet. He is unlikely to be interested in long lists of components that are not used; and how you arrive at your final price is not his concern.

The customer's estimate should be constructed separately on a clear area of the spreadsheet, and should show only what is relevant. You can tackle this in a variety of ways.

One approach would be to group the components of the job and copy across only the sub-total for each set, in the same way that Gross pay, Tax and Net pay were extracted from the Payroll spreadsheet. Here you would give sub-totals for Boiler, Radiators, Cylinders, etc., Pipework and Labour.

An alternative is to use **Lookup** tables to extract information. We will return to these in the next Section.

Preparatory work

Before a job can be costed, it must be defined. It may be possible to do all or part of this on the spreadsheet — that is the case for central heating estimates.

There, the estimator must first work out what size and number of radiators are needed for each room, and what boiler output is needed to cope with the demands of the system. Part of this is done by the spreadsheet shown below. It will calculate the heat requirements in BTUs (British Thermal Units). It does not attempt to give the size and number of radiators as there are some aspects of this that are difficult to quantify — would one big double radiator look and work better than two smaller ones in a particular room? That kind of design question is best left to the human expert.

In the BTU spreadsheet, the thermal requirements of each room are calculated on the basis of the volume of the room, and the target temperature. Adjustments are then made for other factors — the number of outside walls, window area and insulation. As usual, the figures have been simplified to keep the structure clear, but any central heating engineer will be able to add his own improvements.

Only a few formulae are used here.

Cubic feet is, of course, Length * Width * Height

■ SECTION 20
Job costing

	A	B	C	D	E	F	G	H	I
1	B.T.U. Calculations						BTU's		
2	ROOM	LENGTH	WIDTH	HEIGHT	TEMP	CU.FT	Basic	+/- %	Adjusted
3	Hall	14	12	8.5	62	1428	5226	10	5749
4	Lounge	17	15	8.5	65	2168	8726	10	9599
5	Dining	17	14	8.5	65	2023	8145	10	8959
6	Study	10	9	8.5	65	765	3080	10	3388
7	Kitchen	12	10	8.5	65	1020	4107		4107
8	Bed 1	17	15	8	62	2040	7466	10	8213
9	Bed 2	17	14	8	62	1904	6969	10	7666
10	Bed 3	14	12	8	62	1344	4919	30	6395
11	Bed 4	12	12	8	62	1152	4216		4216
12	Bed 5	10	9	8	62	720	2635	10	2899
13	Bath	9	8	8	62	576	2108		2108
14	BOILER SIZE		63298.1						
15									
16	ADJUSTMENT FACTORS					Basic BTU formula			
17	2 outside walls.....+10					F3*(E3-32)*.122			
18	3 outside walls.....+30				Vol * Temp. Gain * constant (.122)				
19	Large windows.......+10								
20	Cavity insulation...-15								

The **Basic** BTU figure is arrived at by the formula:

Volume * Temperature gain * Constant

where the Temperature gain is the difference between the target temperature and 32 degrees F, and the BTU constant is taken as being 0.122. In cell G3, this produces:

F3*(E3-32)*0.122

The **Adjusted** BTU figure takes the percentage in column H into the calculations, so that cell I3 holds:

G3 + H3 % G3

If H3 has a negative value – from insulation – then the adjustment will be downwards.

As with the job costing spreadsheet, this should be saved as a blank, then the copies used for each job should be saved separately. There is no reason why this should not be merged into the central heating sheet, in the same way that the Payroll and Notes sheets were merged into one.

■ SECTION 21
Using Lookup tables

The function **Lookup** will extract values from tables. To use it, you should arrange reference numbers and values in a pair of columns as shown below:

```
    !    A    !!    B    !!    C    !!    D    !!    E    !
 1 !LOOKUP TABLES
 2 !
 3 ! Ref Numbers        Costs
 4 !        1           123.00
 5 !        2           234.00
 6 !        3           345.00   Ref Number          2
 7 !        4           456.00        Cost      234.00
 8 !        5           567.00
 9 !
10 !
```

In this example, the reference number for the relevant item is entered into cell D6. The formula in cell D7 is:

LOOKUP(D6,A4:A8)

This takes the number from D6, and compares it with those in the range A4:A8. When a match is found in Column A, the value in the corresponding cell in Column B is displayed as the **Cost** in D7.

Notes

■ The reference numbers do not have to be a simple sequence — 1,2,3,4,5, ... — but they should be in ascending order. The following list would work perfectly well:

1001
1023
1098
1234
2345

■ You must use numbers for the reference list. You cannot look up the cost of an item by giving its name.

Widget   14.99
Gidget   12.49
Gadget   9.95
Gimble   99.01

Using Lookup tables

Unfortunately, you could not get this kind of lookup table to work — not even if with **textual values** (see below). Numbers must be used.

■ **LOOKUP** does not hunt for an exact match, but instead it looks for the last value that is equal to or less than the given value. This means that a wrongly given reference number will almost certainly find something! It is as well to build some form of cross-checking into the spreadsheet.

■ The value that is looked up must be either a number, or a textual value, i.e. a string enclosed in quotes and brackets, e.g. (''25mm tube''). The text string may not be more than 9 characters long.

■ If you prefer, the LOOKUP tables can be arranged in rows rather than columns. In this case, the reference numbers must be in the upper row; and the values to be looked-up in the row beneath.

Bearing these points in mind, you could construct a set of reference tables to find the description and cost of items on the basis of a reference number.

	A		B		C		D	
10	1001		Blr.43000		1001		220.00	
11	1002		Blr.53000		1002		250.00	
12	1003		Blr.65000		1003		300.00	

If a reference number was written into cell E1, then the formulae:

LOOKUP(E1,A10:A13)
LOOKUP(E1,C10:C13)

would find the description of the required Boiler, and its price. If a fuller and more meaningful description was required, this would have to be spread over two or more tables, and each part of it looked up separately. It will mean more work when setting up the spreadsheet, but costs nothing in user time. The estimator or invoice clerk will still only need to enter a single reference number. SuperCalc3 will do all the donkey work of looking up and displaying the information.

You can see LOOKUP in use in the spreadsheet that is developed in the next section.

■ SECTION 22
Invoice preparation

A number of the ideas that have been introduced over the last few sections are brought together here in the service of Towzers' Fish Sales of Grimsby.

The task

To produce printed invoices for customers, detailing the type and quantity of the fish that have been ordered, with the total costs to show carriage charges and bulk-purchase discounts.

The working data

The types and current prices of fish are shown in the spreadsheet opposite. Carriage is to be charged at 5p per pound. The discount will be 10% on orders over £100, and 15% on orders over £200.

The design

The spreadsheet must be considered in two separate parts — the reference tables and the invoice preparation area. The invoice will occupy the first 20 rows of the sheet; the tables will be sited below. They will therefore not normally be visible when the invoice area is on screen.

The spreadsheet should be arranged so that the salesperson only has to enter the reference number and quantity of each fish type. If need be, the **Window** command can be used to pull the tables into view so that reference numbers may be seen.

The invoice will carry the normal details of supplier and customer, and will list the description, quantity, cost per pound and total cost of each type of fish that is ordered — up to a maximum of seven lines. (Few of Towzers' customers deal in more than four types of fish. Seven is a realistic maximum.) Discount and carriage calculations will also be shown.

When the invoice is complete, it can be printed by the **Output** command. A second copy can be taken for the firm's use, or the spreadsheet could be saved to serve as a copy:

The lookup tables are arranged in two pairs of columns, with reference numbers in columns A and C, descriptions in B and prices in D. You will notice that the descriptions have been compressed so that they fit the nine character limit for textual values. The column has been formatted to justify the text to the left. Textual values — like number values — are right-justified by default.

```
     :  A  ::    B  ::   C  ::   D  ::   E  :
 1:TOWZERS FISH SALES
 2:Tel. Grimsby 123456
 3:
 4:Invoice to:........JAKE'S FISHERIES
 5:Fish Ref Type      Quantity Unit Cost Amount
 6: 1       Large Cod    25.00    1.45    36.25
 7: 2       Small Cod    50.00    1.20    60.00
 8: 4       Smk.Haddk    10.00    1.70    17.00
 9: 6       Plaice       40.00    1.40    56.00
10: 8       Shrimps      25.00    1.90    47.50
11: 10      Mussels      25.00    1.58    39.50
12:                        .00      .00      .00
13:                            Sub-total  256.25
14:                   Discount   15.00    38.44
15:                            TOTAL     217.81
16:                            WEIGHT    175.00
17:                            CARRIAGE    8.75
18:                            ------------------
19:                            TO PAY    226.56
```

Remember when using textual values that they must be given in brackets and quotes. Thus, the Entry line for cell B23 looked like this:

    11>("Large cod") _

```
               :  A  ::    B  ::   C  ::   D  :
21:LOOK UP TABLES
22:Ref No    Type        Ref No   Price
23: 1        Large Cod      1      1.45
24: 2        Small Cod      2      1.20
25: 3        Haddock        3      1.40
26: 4        Smk.Haddk      4      1.70
27: 5        Coley          5       .90
28: 6        Plaice         6      1.40
29: 7        Mackerel       7       .95
30: 8        Shrimps        8      1.90
31: 9        Crab live      9      2.50
32: 10       Mussels       10      1.58
33:
34:Carriage (p.lb)               .05
```

■ SECTION 22
Invoice preparation

Calculations and formulae

Each item line of the invoice takes this shape:

```
 !  A  !!        B       !!  C  !!       D        !!  E  !
5!Fish Ref Type                Quantity Unit Cost            Amount
6!(value)    LOOKUP(A6,A23:A32) (value)    LOOKUP(A6,C23:C32) C6*D6
```

The **Type** LOOKUP serves as a check that the right reference number is given.

The **Discount** formula may be expressed in this way:

> If the TOTAL is more than £200, then the discount is 15%; IF the TOTAL is more than £100 the discount is 10%, otherwise there is no discount.

With the TOTAL value in D13, this produces the formula:

IF(D13>200,15,IF(D13>100,10,0))

It is not necessary in the second part of the formula to check that the total is less than £200. If it wasn't, then SuperCalc3 would have already allocated a discount of 15% and moved onto the next cell of the spreadsheet.

More Lookups, less typing

The more data that can be held in lookup tables, the less typing is needed in preparing the invoices. The extra time that is spent in setting it all up could be recouped very quickly.

If the firm deals with a limited set of customers, then their names, addresses and other details could also be held in lookup tables. The nine character limit will cause problems in setting up the spreadsheet as names and addresses will need to be chopped into small chunks. However, as long as the customer detail cells in the invoice area are all nine characters wide, the pieces will fit together neatly for printouts.

A firm that gives different discounts to customers depending upon long-term factors, rather than the quantity purchased at any particular time, might usefully include the discounts in a lookup table.

■ SECTION 23
Stock control

A spreadsheet can be used very efficiently for stock control. With a little care and forethought, you can design one that will work as well as any special-purpose stock control software that you can buy. What's more, the flexibility of SuperCalc3 means that you can tailor the sheet to suit your stock system, rather than having to alter your system to suit a ready-made package.

A bare skeleton of a stock control spreadsheet is shown below:

```
    !  A   !!  B   !!  C   !!  D   !!  E    !!  F     !!  G    !!  H   !
 1 !STOCK CONTROL
 2 !Type     Current  Qty OUT  Qty IN   Updated  Minimum  Reorder  Cost
 3 !Widgets       2       1             5        6        5            2.50
 4 !Gidgets       5              12    17       10            4.00
 5 !Gadgets       4       2             2        5   REORDER  10.00
 6 !Gimbles      30       5            25       25             .50
 7 !Watnots     285      40           245      250   REORDER   .35
 8 !
 9 !
10 !Total Stock Value    201.25
11 !
```

All this does is keep track of the numbers in stock, and their cost prices. Realistically, it should also record selling prices, suppliers' details or references, re-order time, location of items, previous year's sales and sales-to-date − amongst other things. It could also be linked directly to an invoicing module like the one outlined in the previous section.

The STOCK spreadsheet has been kept simple so that we can focus on a particular problem − that of updating a spreadsheet. Those developed so far have been once-only sheets. With stock control, we have to pass values on from one use to the next. A little example will show the problem more clearly.

The key columns in this kind of spreadsheet are those where we record the quantities in stock and the changes:

```
      !  A   !!  B   !!  C   !!  D   !
 2 !
 3 !ITEM     OUT      IN       Quantity
 4 !Widgets   12       5       ????
```

Stock control

What goes in cell D3? At first sight, the answer would appear to be **D3 +
C3 − B3**. But if you do that, the value will change every time the
spreadsheet is recalculated. If at the start of the working session, D3 held
25, it will be changed first to 18 (25 + 5-12 = 18) then to 11 next time the
sheet is recalculated, then down to 4 and so on.

You can switch off the automatic recalculation with the
/G(lobal),M(anual) command. Then the calculations will only be
performed when you press the ! key − but what would happen in
practice? You would have clear the OUT and IN columns before you
started, so that previous entries did not get in the way; then enter all the
changes − without mistakes or omissions − before calling up the
calculation. All in all, a cumbersome and error-prone process.

So what is the solution? If you look at the illustration above, you will see
that there are four columns concerned with quantity − **Current, Qty
OUT, Qty IN,** and **Updated.** The **Current** column holds the stock levels at
the start of the working session. The **Updated** column has formulae of the
type − **B3 − C3 + D3** − simple arithmetic to take the OUT and IN values
into account.

Now, to use this properly, you must transfer all the values from the
Updated to the **Current** column at the start of each session, then clear the
OUT and IN columns before you begin entering the new changes. It can
be done with these two commands (assuming that the column letters and
active ranges are the same as those in the illustration above, i.e.

/Copy,**E3:E8,B3,V**alues
/Blank,**C3:D8**

The **Values** option at the end of the Copy command makes SuperCalc3
transfer only the values, and not the formulae, from the source cells.

If the stock updating is to be done by junior, or inexperienced staff, and
there is the possibility that they may not be able to cope with the
command sequence adequately − and remember that this is a grossly
simplified system − then the whole process can be automated. We will
return to this in the next section, 'Spreadsheets without tears'.

Re-order levels

Any stock control software worth its salt (on chips?) should give the user
warning when stock levels fall below the minimum. This can be catered
for quite easily by the spreadsheet.

■ SECTION 23
Stock control

With column E holding the Updated stock levels and the minimum numbers being written into column F, a formula of this type will alert the user of low stocks:

IF(E3<F3,"REORDER","")

As an alternative to the blank cell that will be produced by the pair of quotes, the formula could show the number above minimum, if any. Blank cells would make the occasional "REORDER" stand out more clearly, but the surplus quantity might be worth knowing.

Running totals

Keeping track of usage rates with the month-to-date and year-to-date figures will add significantly to the efficiency of the stock system.

Monthly usage can be handled in much the same way as the day-to-day updating. You will need two columns, one with the current month-to-date figures, the other to hold formulae of the type **Current + Quantity OUT**. The sales recorded in each working session – and used elsewhere to update stock levels – are reused here to update the monthly figures. As with the regular update, the latest figures would need to be transferred into the current column at the start of each working session.

For the year-to-date figures, it may be better to set aside an area of the spreadsheet to hold the figures for each month, and the annual totals. You would then have a special End of the Month session with the worksheet in which the figures for the current month would be copied out of the month-to-date column and into the appropriate one in the year's summary section. The month-to-date columns would then need to be zeroed ready for the new month:

```
   :  I   ::  J   ::  K   ::  L  : ..... :  X  :
1 |MONTH-TO-DATE
2|Current  Updated  JAN     FEB            YEAR TOTAL
3|(copied  I3+C3   (copied from J at       SUM(K3:V3)
4|daily)            end of month)
```

■ SECTION 23
Stock control

Alternative layouts?

The Stock spreadsheet has been organised so that each type of item occupies a single row. Would it work better if it was laid out column-wise? With 20 lines to the screen, most − if not all − of the figures relating to an item could be seen at once. Printouts would also be easier, for any spreadsheet that is more than 8 or 10 columns wide will have to be printed in strips, and matching up the strips can be fiddly.

In fact, there are two very good reasons for selecting the row-wise arrangement. First, it allows you to handle far more items − there are 254 rows but only 62 columns. Secondly, data must be organised into rows if you are to take advantage of SuperCalc3's data management commands, and these could be useful in a stock control spreadsheet.

We will return to data management in Sections 43 to 47. Meanwhile, let's have a look at ways of making spreadsheets easier to use.

SuperCalc3 has the ability to accept pre-programmed command sequences via the /eXecute command. To use this, you must first create a file in which your commands are written – just as they would be entered from the keyboard. The **eXecute** command will then work its way through the sequence, performing each of the filed commands in turn. Control can be passed back and forth between the user and the eXecute file.

Let's see what this means in practice. Consider the Stock spreadsheet. A normal working session would involve the following sequence of events:

1. Clear any previous spreadsheet.
2. Load in the STOCK file.
3. Copy the values in the Updated to the Current column.
4. Blank the OUT and IN columns.
5. Enter the new stock movements.
6. Save the updated sheet.

Most of that can be translated into a series of commands.

1. /**Z**ap,**Y**es
2. /**L**oad,**STOCK,A**ll
3. /**C**opy,**E3:E8,B3,V**alues
4. /**B**lank,**C3:D8**
5. * * * Keyboard Use * * *
6. /**S**ave,**STOCK,B**ackup,**A**ll

Extract from those characters shown in bold type – the keystrokes that are actually made – and we are more than half-way towards making an eXecute file.

If you have created your own Stock Control file, make a note of the cell references of the Current, Out, In and Updated columns; save it and Zap the spreadsheet. If you didn't make one, then copy the one at the beginning of the previous Section. For this purpose it is enough to write the area from A1 to E8 only. Save it as "Stock" and Zap clear.

An eXecute file can be written on any word processor that can produce pure text files, but it is often simpler to use SuperCalc3. To do this, Format column A so that it is wide enough to take the longest command that will be written in the file; 20 characters will be more than sufficient usually. Now use the /**Global,Border** command to remove the row and column displays. They are not needed and will corrupt the execute file.

The commands should be written down column A, starting at the top, and to make the commands actually appear on the spreadsheet, (rather

than being performed) you must make SuperCalc3 treat them as text by
starting each entry with quotes. Write only those characters that would
be actually typed in the commands − this may include some punctuation:

```
"/ZY
"/LSTOCK,A          (include the comma)
"/CE3:E8,B3,V        (commas and colon!)
"/BC3:D8
&                   (note the ampersand)
"/SSTOCK,B,A
```

Note the & (ampersand) in the fifth line. This tells the **eXecute** command
to pass control back to the keyboard. The user will then return control to
eXecute by typing an ampersand when the keyboard work is done.

Check that your sheet looks like the list of commands above with
whatever amendments are necessary to suit your own stock control
spreadsheet, then save this file − twice. Save it once with the /**Save**
command, so that it can be loaded back again for any editing if need be:

/Save,**STOCKEX,A**ll

Save it a second time with the /**Output** command. This time add a .**XQT**
ending to the filename so that the eXecute command will be able to
recognise it as a command file:

/Output,Display,**A1:A6,D**isk,**STOCKEX.XQT**

(You might like to check the disk directory afterwards to make sure that
the files are there. You should be able to see: 'STOCK.CAL' − the
spreadsheet; 'STOCKEX.CAL' - the editing copy; and 'STOCKEX.XQT'
− the command file.)

Now test it. Call up the eXecute command, and give it the filename
'STOCKEX'. Don't bother with the .XQT ending at this point. SuperCalc3
will look for it anyway.

/**X**ecute,**STOCKEX**

You will see the commands appear in the Entry line as they are executed
− though there will scarcely be time to read some of them. When the
eXecute command reaches the & it will display this message in the
Prompt line:

Awaiting keyboard entry

The user now has full control − just as normal. He or she can enter data,

Spreadsheets without tears

write new formulae, extend and adapt the sheet, reFormat the display, Output a printer copy, or whatever. Any command can be used — including another **eXecute**.

Control is returned to **eXecute** when the user types an ampersand. The next item in the command file will then appear in the Entry line as it is performed.

EXecute in everyday use

EXecute can do much to simplify the daily spreadsheet work. By taking care of all essential commands, it can leave the user free to concentrate on the data entry. But the execute file can also handle data entry if this is required. Anything that can be written in the Entry line can be included in an execute file. Thus, you can move the spreadsheet cursor to a particular cell with the = function, then write the text, formula or value that is to go there:

```
/ZY
=A1
Spring
Summer
Autumn
Winter
Year
=E2
SUM(A2:D2)
/RE2,E3:E10
=A2
&
```

This file will first clear the spreadsheet, then write the headings **Spring, Summer, Autumn, Winter, Year** across cells A1 to E1. The spreadsheet cursor is then moved to E2, where the formula **SUM(A2:D2)** is written. This is **R**eplicated from E2 to the range E3:10, before the cursor is moved back to A2 to await keyboard entry.

In theory, you could create a whole spreadsheet using an eXecute file. In practice, of course, it is easier to do it directly on the screen. You should, however, think about creating an eXecute file wherever you find that you are regularly performing the same sequence of operations. It will save time, and reduce errors.

File management

There are a number of aspects to files and disk use that have been touched on in the last few sections, and that will become more important as we delve deeper into SuperCalc3. Now is perhaps a good time to look more closely at those commands that handle files.

You can **Save** files in any of four ways.

The **All** option saves the entire spreadsheet, complete with formulae. This will be the most commonly used way.

Values comes into its own where you are using a single spreadsheet with different sets of figures. The Budget sheet, for example, could be reused for further six-month periods. Save one copy of the spreadsheet complete with its formulae,and the rest as values only. The value sheets will take less disk space.

Part will save a section of the sheet, defined by the cell references of its upper left and lower right cell references. Partial saves are normally used where you intend to merge some data from one sheet into another.

Before you are asked for the cell range, SuperCalc3 will prompt for **All** or **Values**. The All is slightly misleading − what it wants to know is whether to save formulae or not. Make your choice, then complete the command with the cell references.

The **Load** command has a more extensive range of options.

All simply loads in exactly what was saved, and overwrites the current spreadsheet. Any blank cells on the new spreadsheet will allow the old sheet's contents − if any − to show through. You would normally use the **Zap** command before loading to avoid corruption, but there may be times when you want to merge spreadsheets this way.

The **P**art option gives a very flexible means of combining two spreadsheets. It can take in a section − or all − of a second sheet and relocate it anywhere within the first sheet. It is most commonly used to bring totals from subsidiary sheets − departmental or monthly analyses perhaps − into an overall summary sheet. We have already noted its ability to merge separately developed modules into a single working sheet (*c.f.* Notes and Payroll).

This option works very similarly to the Copy command. The part to load is defined by giving the cell references of the upper left and lower right corners − and if the whole sheet is wanted, then these references will be A1 and the **Last Col/Row** cell. The place on the sheet in which it is to be copied is specified by the upper left cell.

File management

The normal Copying options are there. Give the command in its simplest form:

Load,filename,**Part,C1:D10,F1** <RETURN>

and the cell references will be automatically adjusted, as the section is moved from one range to another.

Type a comma after giving the ranges, and you can select from

N(o adjust), A(sk for Adjust), V(alues), +, −, *, /

The artithmetic operators (+, −, *, /) would be used where the values on the second sheet are to be combined with those of the existing sheet.

The **Consolidate** option is the second method of combining sheets. In consolidation, the values in the cells of the second sheet are added to those in the existing sheet. Normally the two sheets will share a common layout and set of formulae. It might be used, for example, where the same basic design was used for the spreadsheet that collects the daily figures and the one that keeps the on-going totals. At the end of the day, the daily sheet would be consolidated into the permanent sheet.

Output to disk

Files can be created using the **Output** command, but they are not of the same type as those created with **Save**.

When you **Output** a spreadsheet − or more usually, part of one − to disk, then it is stored as a text file. This is, of course, the way that most word processors handle their files − so that Outputting to disk can be a very convenient way of incorporating spreadsheet material into written reports. It is also, as we noted in the last section, the way to create eXecute files.

■ SECTION 25
File management

Output to WordStar

If you are writing a report with WordStar, or a similar word processor, and want to include a spreadsheet display in it, you can manage it quite simply with SuperCalc3.

1 Load in the relevant spreadsheet, and determine the part of the sheet that you want to include in your report.

2 Put the disk containing your WordStar text files into the disk drive. You will have problems with WordStar if you try to merge files that are on different disks.

3 Switch off the Row and Column display with the /Global, Border command – unless you want the border!

4 Call up the Output command, select the Display mode amd define the range that you want to save; then take the Disk option. Give the filename, but do not include an extension unless your word processor demands one. SuperCalc3 will automatically add a .PRN extension to the name, and most word processors will accept this:

/Output, Display, range, Disk, filename

PART FIVE

Graphs

All of SuperCalc3's graphing facilities are handled via the /**View** command. As there are a lot of facilities, this command is inevitably quite complicated. Fortunately, you can produce some very respectable results without going into **View** to any great depth.

First of all, you need some figures to graph. The examples in this section are all based on the Budget spreadsheet in its six-month version, as shown here:

```
      A    !!  B    !!   C  !!  D  !!  E  !!  F  !!  G  !!  H  !
 1!BUDGET    First Half
 2!          January February March    April    May     June    Totals
 3!Income 1     800      800      800      800     800     800    4800
 4!Income 2     200      200      200      200     200     200    1200
 5!Total In    1000     1000     1000     1000    1000    1000    6000
 6!
 7!House        240      200      200      240     240     240    1360
 8!Food         200      200      200      200     200     200    1200
 9!Fuel          80       80       80       60      60      60     420
10!Clothes       60       20       60       40      60      60     300
11!Car          100      250      100      100     170     100     820
12!Computer      50       50       50       50      50       0     250
13!Miscellan    200       60      190      120     100     200     870
14!
15!TOTAL OUT    930      860      880      810     880     860    5220
16!
17!Saving!       70      140      120      190     120     140     780
18!
19!        J        F        M        A        M        J
20!        IN      OUT     SAVE
```

(You may notice some extraneous material in Rows 19 and 20. The purpose of this will become clear as we go on.)

Load up your own version of Budget. It is a good spreadsheet for demonstrating many aspects of graphs.

■ SECTION 26
The View command

The basic graph

Call up the /**View** command and look at the Prompt line.

#,?,D(ata),G(raph-Type),T(ime-Labs),V(ar-Labs),P(oint-Labs), H(eads) or O(pts)

For the moment, we can forget everything but the first option, for the only thing that SuperCalc3 *must* have if it is to produce a graph is some **data** to work on. Press **D** to bring you to this position:

Var A: Enter range (now empty), <space> to skip, <-> to clear
14>/View,1,Data,__

You might notice that a **1** has appeared in the Entry line. This is because you are working on Graph No.1 − SuperCalc3 will always start with this unless you instruct it otherwise. We will return to the subject of graph numbers in Section 28.

The **Data range** is the row or column of numbers that are to be graphed. Up to 10 different ranges − identified as Variables A through to J − can be included in a single graph. Here we are working on **Variable A** − note the start of the prompt line. Give it the range B5:G5, or the equivalent from your sheet, to show Total In.

Press RETURN, and note that the Entry line is still displaying the /**View,__** start. When a View option has been completed, control returns to the start of the View command, rather than dropping back to the spreadsheet level. SuperCalc3 is waiting for a further View option. Exit by pressing RETURN again, and the graph that you are working on will be displayed as the command ends. Try it.

If your Total In figures are as regular as the ones in the example sheet, you should now have a rather pointless bar graph showing a set of bars of exactly the same height! Let's add a bit of interest to this, by using the graph to show the patterns of Income, Expenditure and Saving. Call up View again, and select the Data option. Look again at that prompt line.

Var A: Enter range (B5:G5), <space> to skip, <-> to clear

14>/View,1,Data,__

Data entry always starts at Variable A. We are happy with the range (B5:G5) that we are using there, so move onto the next by pressing <space>. For Variable B, give the range B15:G15, or whatever references for Total Out, and press the **comma** key rather than RETURN. You will then be prompted for Variable C's range. Give it as B17:G17 (or equivalent) — the Savings figures. You could press comma again to define the next variable, but three will be enough here, so exit from the Data section by pressing RETURN.

When you get back to the start position (/View,___), press RETURN again to see the latest version of the graph. It should look something like this:

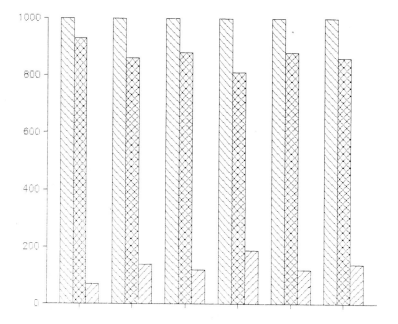

What does it mean? It's rather difficult to tell without any headings or annotations. Let's find out how to add these to the display.

Call up the /**View** command again. We will use some more of the options shown in the Prompt line to improve the appearance of our first graph.

   #;?,D(ata),G(raph-Type),T(ime-Labs),V(ar-Labs),P(oint-Labs), H(eads) or O(pts)

Press **T** to select the Time-Labels options. You will be prompted to enter the Time-Label range. Any labels or headings that are to appear on the graph must be written somewhere on the spreadsheet, as the SuperCalc3 graph functions can only work with information that is in cells.

The Time-Labels always refer to the labels that go across the bottom of the graph. Often, as in this case, the horizontal axis does represent time. The labels we want here are the month names. Enter B2:G2, or your own equivalent, to give the range that covers 'January' to 'June'. Press RETURN twice to exit from this section and display the graph.

You should see a rather dramatic change in the size of your graph. Those long Time-Labels have taken up a lot of screen space. There are a couple of ways to chop them down to a more reasonable size — and allow the graph to expand again. Probably the simplest way is to add another line to the spreadsheet, giving the labels as you would like them to appear in the graph. If you look back to the first figure in the previous section, you will see that the months' initials are written in the range B19:G19.

Key in the months' initials or abbreviations on your sheet, then return to the Time-Label section of View and give the new cell range. You will find that where short labels are used, they are displayed horizontally, but that longer ones are written down the screen. Try different label lengths and observe their effect on the presentation. You do not need to go through the View routine unless you need to alter the range. Simply press **F10** to display the current graph.

Var-Labs is the next option to explore. The Variable Labels will appear on a bar graph as a legend down the right-hand side. As with the Time-Labels, the longer they are, the less room there will be available for the graph itself. For this reason, the labels **IN, OUT** and **SAVE** have been written into cells B20:D20 of the sample spreadsheet. These references need to be given to View. Call it up and select **Var-Labs**. You will be prompted:

   Var A: Var-Label cell or range (now empty), <space> to skip, <-> to clear

There are two ways to get all three references in. Either press the **comma** key after entering each individual cell reference so that you work through Var B and Var C; or enter all three at once as a range — **B20:D20**. SuperCalc3 will allocate the three cells in the range to the three variables. (Obviously, you can only use the range method where the labels are all in adjacent cells and in the right order!)

Let's add Headings to this graph before we leave it and move onto something new. Select the **H(eads)** option. You will be prompted:

M(ain), S(ub), X(-axis) or Y(-axis)?

You will need to give a cell reference for each of the headings that you use, but — unlike the Variable Label routine — you cannot give a range of four cells to cover the lot. Each must be given separately. On the sample sheet in the previous section you will see 'Budget' in A1, and 'First Half' in B1. These can be used as the Main and Sub-headings. Give the references, and view the result. You should now have something not unlike this:

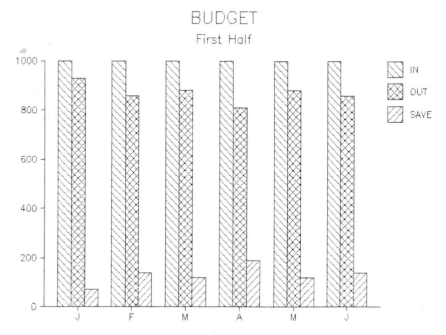

If you want a printout of your graph, and you have a suitable printer or plotter, then simply press **F9** to output it to paper.

To retain the graph for future reference, **/Save** the spreadsheet again. Graphs are automatically saved as part of the process. Check the directory, with the **See .CAL files** option, and you will find the graph listed below the spreadsheet's details.

■ SECTION 28
Selecting graph types

Call up **/View** and press **G**, to get the **Graph-Types** option; then work through the selection, viewing each one in turn, by pressing RETURN twice after choosing.

P(ie), B(ar), S(tacked-Bar), L(ine), H(i-Lo), X(-Y) or A(rea)?

It should be fairly obvious that different types of graphs have different uses. With the particular set of data that we are using at the moment, a bar or stacked bar graph will give pleasing results, but some of the others look most odd. How should they be used?

Pie graphs

These are used where you only want to show the breakdown of one variable into its components. It might be Annual Sales broken down by stock type; contributions to gross profit by departments; or − to take an example from the Budget spreadsheet − Expenditure by category. Let's work on that, as we have the figures at hand.

Call up **/View**, and this time, notice the hash sign # at the start of the prompt line. That is there to remind you that you can have up to nine graphs associated with any single spreadsheet, and that you can specify them by number. We have already defined Graph #1, so let's select the next. Type **2**. From now on, until you specify a different graph number, the number 2 will always appear whenever you use the View command.

The **Data** range must be defined before we can do anything with a graph. Give the range G7:G13, or the equivalent to pick out the Totals for House, Food, Fuel and other items of expenditure. *Don't* include the overall TOTAL OUT figure.

/View,2,Data,G7:G13

Return to the View prompt and select Pie chart from the Graph-Type options. Press F10 to view. You will see that SuperCalc3 has automatically added the figures to show the percentage value of each segment of the pie.

Headings and Labels are specified here just as they are with bar charts, but note these important differences in the way that they are positioned around the chart.

The **Variable-Label** − there will only ever be one on a pie chart − will appear at the bottom of the display, as a kind of sub-heading.

The **Time-Labels** identify the segments of the pie. They will be displayed down the right-hand side, as Variable Labels are on other charts. It is important to keep them reasonably succinct as the pie shrinks alarmingly when long labels are used.

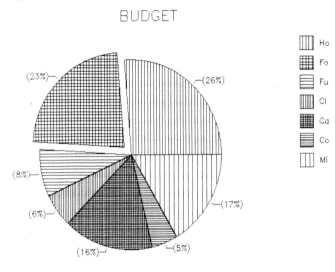

BUDGET

Totals

More than one variable

A pie chart can only show the breakdown of one variable at a time, but there is nothing to stop you producing pie charts of many variables – one at a time. We could do that here, to produce a pie chart for each month, and it won't take much effort either.

Start by going back to the **Data** routine, and with the Prompt line showing the current range of Var A, type in the references of the top left and bottom right cells of the whole block – from January's 'House' to June's 'Miscellaneous'.

Press RETURN, then go back into the **Data** routine again and look at the ranges that it shows for the variables. You should see that Var A has a range B5:B13 (or equivalent), Var B has C5:C13, and so on. SuperCalc3 has taken the block reference and divided it into separate variable ranges.

When you give a block range, SuperCalc3 will split it into variables on the basis of length. If the block has more columns than rows, it is assumed that the variables run across the rows. In this example, there were 6 columns and 7 rows. The months were therefore taken as being the variables. The block will retain that organisation even if you reduce the number of rows afterwards.

Specify the cells containing the months as your Variable labels, then look at your current graph by pressing **F10**. It should show the breakdown of expenditure in January. To look at the other months, you will need to go into the /**View** command and select **O(pts)**. The options that you have are:

F(ormat), E(xplosion), P(ie-Mode) or S(caling)

Press **P** for Pie-Mode, and you will be asked if you want **O**(ne Variable) or **A**(ll Variables). Opt for **One**, and it will ask 'Which one?' offering you A to J. In this particular example you have defined ranges for the six variables A through to F, so any of those may be selected. Try a few of them, perhaps outputting some to paper so that you can compare them, then get back to the **Pie-Mode** level with the sequence:

/View,2,Options,Pie-Mode,

This time, select **All Variables**. This will not give you a multiple pie display – which is a shame because there are times when one would be useful. What it does do is give you the facility to compare the same point, or element, across the variables. In other words, it redivides the data block the opposite way. Here, it means that it will produce pie charts that show the expenditure on any single category over the six-month period.

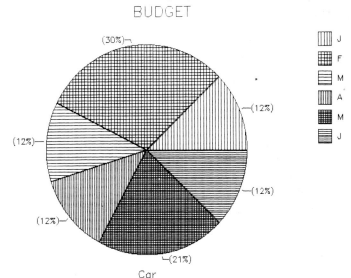

Selecting graph types

Pick a point to plot – you will be offered 1 to 254, but only the first seven should have any data in this instance – and see what the results look like. If you regularly spend the same, or similar, amounts in any given category each month, then these displays are likely to have limited value. However, there may be situations where this kind of cross-analysis by pie charts could be useful.

Don't forget that you can always change your graph style without having to redefine variables and labels. Try it now, and select a stacked bar display for that block of variables. As you will see, this kind of graph is far better suited for showing change over time than any kind of pie chart.

Line graphs

Line graphs are good for showing trends. It is far easier to follow the shape and slope of a line than to work out the relationships between sequences of figures in a table, or even between the varying heights of bars in a bar chart.

In this section we will look at line, area and X-Y graph types, using this sample spreadsheet:

```
 !  A  !!  B  !!  C  !!  D  !!  E  !!  F  !
1!SALES AND EXPENSES
2!       Jan     Feb    March   April    May
3!Widgets   3000    8000   12000   10000    7000
4!Gadgets   5000    5000    5000    5000    5000
5!Thingies  2000    2000    3000    2500    1000
6!
7!Sales    10000   15000   20000   17500   13000
8!Expenses   125     125     300     200     150
9!
```

Zap the spreadsheet clear and key in the Sales as shown – use your own choice of item names if you don't fancy the Widget business. The figures given here are all round numbers to make them easier to copy. You may prefer to make them more realistic, but don't alter them by more than a few pounds either way.

Now call up /**View,1,Data,** and specify the range B3:F5. This should allocate B3:F3 to Var A, B4:F4 to Var B and B5:F5 to Var C. Select **Line** for the Graph-Type and view the result:

■ SECTION 28
Selecting graph types

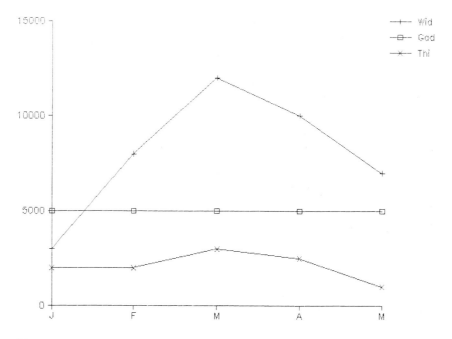

You should see that the graph displays, very clearly, that the Gadget sales are regular; that after a brief peak, the Thingy sales are tailing off; and that Widgets have become the leading item − but that the sales trend is downwards there as well.

Now switch to a bar chart display and look at the graph again. The trends are still visible, but are they as clear as in a line graph?

Area graphs

This is another form of line graph, but here the lines are plotted above each other to give cumulative totals. They are called area graphs because it is the area between each pair of lines that is significant, rather than the actual position of the lines.

Select **Area** from the Graph-Types. Your graph should be the same as that below. You will note that Var A has been plotted first and as normal, but that Var B's figures have been added to those of the corresponding points of A and plotted above them. The line for Var C, at the top, is thus equivalent to the totals for all three.

A stacked bar graph will give a similar display, as it also adds each

113

Selecting graph types

variable to the previous one before plotting. Try it, and compare the two. As with the earlier line and bar comparisons, you should find that the area graph gives a better idea of the trends.

X – Y graphs

These are used where you want to find the relationship – if any – between two sets of figures. In the Sales example, we would like to know if there is a correlation between Sales and Expenses. (As these figures are so simple, the correlation is fairly obvious anyway, but in real life you are less likely to have nice round numbers to work with!)

Set up a new graph, and specify B7:F7 for Variable A, and B8:F8 for Variable B. View it as a bar chart:

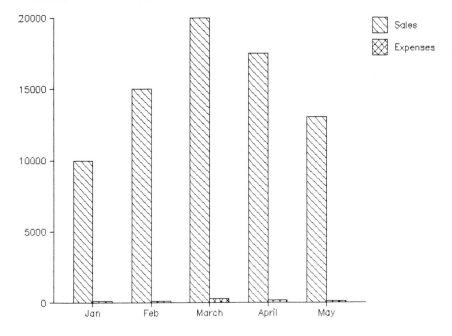

The difference in scale between the Sales and Expense figures is so large that the Expenses are virtually invisible. A line display will be equally uninformative.

Select the **X – Y** Graph Type and look again:

■ SECTION 28
Selecting graph types

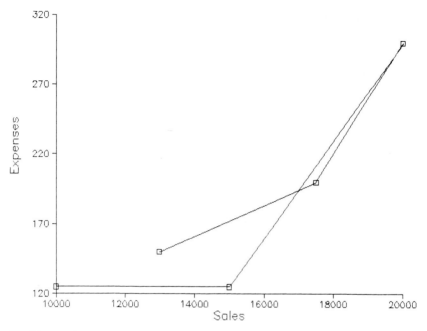

X – Y graphs are quite unlike any of the others. Here, the values of Variable A are used as the X-axis, and those of Variable B as the Y-axis. Each pair of points is plotted in turn, then joined to the next with a line.

The closer the relationship between the two sets of figures, the straighter the line will be. You can see this by altering the figures in the spreadsheet.

Try it first with a fixed relationship between the two sets.

Sales	10000	15000	20000	17500	13000
Expenses	100	150	200	175	130

This will give a solid diagonal line on the graph. The correlation is absolute.

Try it with more random figures

Sales	10000	15000	20000	17500	13000
Expenses	500	250	100	400	200

The zig-zag lines over the resulting graph tell you that there is no correlation between the sets of figures.

Go back to the original values for Expenses (or look at the last figure above), and you should be able to tell that there is some correlation between the sets. Expenses do rise with Sales, though not on a fixed basis. In the real world, an approximate correlation is all you would ever normally expect to find.

Hi-Lo graphs

The **Hi-Lo** graph is ideally suited for displaying the range and movement of share prices or exchange rates. To use it, the highest values for each day, or week, must be given in Variable A, and the lowest in Variable B. These will then be plotted as the top and bottom points of vertical lines. If other variables are also included, then they will be plotted on those lines. The following two illustrations show a typical set of figures and the Hi-Lo graph produced by them.

```
    ¦     A    ¦¦  B  ¦¦  C  ¦¦  D  ¦¦  E  ¦¦  F  ¦
1¦HILO
2¦Dollar rates 2 /1     9 /1    16/1    23/1    30/1
3¦Highest        1.485   1.475   1.49   1.5135   1.519
4¦Lowest         1.4725  1.4655  1.47   1.4955   1.5005
5¦Closing        1.482   1.468   1.477  1.512    1.515
```

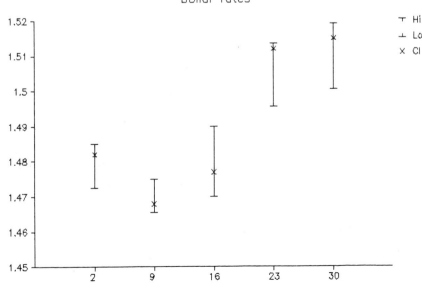

HILO

Dollar rates

■ SECTION 29
Further View options

Over the last four sections we have covered the most significant aspects of the View command. There are a few remaining options that can be used to improve presentation of your graphs. Let's have a look at those now.

The main /**View** prompt line shows these options:

   #,?,D(ata),G(raph-Type),T(ime-Labs),V(ar-Labs),P(oint-Labs), H(eads) or O(pts)

Note the ? near the beginning of the line. Press the ? key, and instead of the usual Help screen, you will get a description of your current graph. It is a useful summary of the graph, but is information only. You cannot change anything except through the View options.

```
Current Graph (#4) --> Stacked-Bar       Current Device --> IBM Graphics
                                                                 Printer
HEADINGS:                      SCALING:
Main:    (D1)                  Y-Axis: Auto
Sub:     (empty)               X-Axis: Auto
X-Axis: (empty)
Y-Axis: (empty)


TIME LABELS: (B2:G2)

      Data         Pt-Labels      Var-Labels      FORMATS:
A: (B7:G7)         (empty)        (A7)            Axis:
B: (B8:G8)         (empty)        (A8)            Time: Width = 3
C: (B9:G9)         (empty)        (A9)            Var: Width = 3
D: (B10:G10)       (empty)        (A10)           Point:
E: (B11:G11)       (empty)        (A11)           % :
F: (B12:G12)       (empty)        (A12)
G: (B13:G13)       (empty)        (A13)
H: (empty)         (empty)        (empty)
I: (empty)         (empty)        (empty)
J: (empty)         (empty)        (empty)

PIE EXPLOSION: None              MODE: All Variables (3)
F1 or <?> for AnswerScreen.
F1 = Help; F2 = Erase Line/Return to Spreadsheet; F9 = Plot; F10 = View
```

Further along the Prompt line you will find **P(oint-Labs)**. Select this if you want to have the point values or labels written on the tops of bars or the markers on line graphs. If you want the values to be shown, then use the same cell range for the Point-Labels that you are using for the variables. Otherwise give the references of the cells with the appropriate labels in them.

We looked briefly at the **O(pts)** earlier when we were exploring pie charts. They are well worth a second look.

   F(ormat), E(xplosion), P(ie-Mode) or S(caling)?

■ SECTION 29
Further View options

Format   This will allow you to format the figures and text that appear on the displays, in just the same way that they can be formatted in the spreadsheet. This means, for example, that you can clip long labels down to an acceptable size by giving them a width of a few characters, and that money figures can be displayed in the $ format.

A(xis), T(ime), V(ar), P(oint) or % labels
24>View,2,Options,Format,___

You can Format the Axes, Time-, Variable- or Point-Labels and also the percentages on the pie charts. Select the % sign for this latter one. The percentages are normally shown as whole numbers in brackets, e.g. **(23%)**. This requires a format width of five characters. Cut down to three to remove the brackets; any less will suppress the display completely. The fewer characters used in the display, the larger the pie chart can be.

Explosion   This option allows you to highlight some or all of the segments in a pie chart. In the following illustration, three segments were selected for explosion.

Highlight Pie Segments? A(ll), N(one) or <1-8> (segment #)
33>View,2,Options,Explosions,1,4,7,<RETURN>

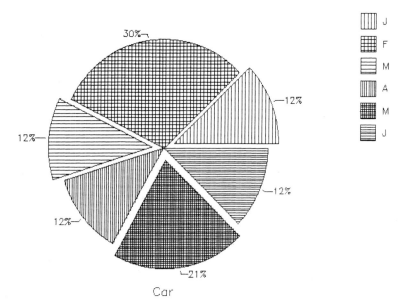

■ SECTION 29
Further View options

Scaling This option should be used where the automatic scaling is not to your liking. Suppose you have a variable range like this:

	B		C		D		E		F		G	
2	95000		100000		92000		97000		90000		93000	

SuperCalc3 is intelligent in its scaling. With this kind of range it will assume that you do not want the Y-axis to run from 0 to 100,000, and will pitch the base figure a little below the lowest in the range.

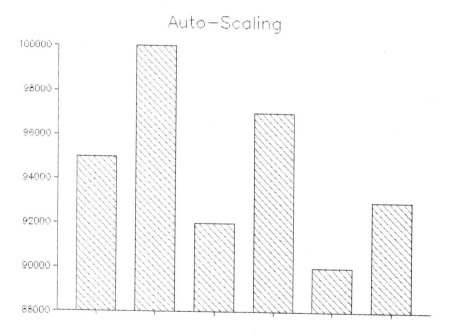

Auto—Scaling

If you want to drop the base to a lower point — perhaps to emphasise that sales have stayed high, even though there has been some variation — then select the Scaling option, and pick the **Y-axis**.

Enter Cell containing Minimum, or <space> for Auto-Scaling.
31>View,2,Options,Scaling,Y-axis, ‗

As always, SuperCalc3 works only from cell references, so the base figure must be written into the sheet somewhere if it is not there at present. We will slot '0' in cell B3.

> Cell containing Maximum?
> 34>View,2,Options,Scaling,Y-axis,B3, ___

Again, give the reference of the highest value cell, or of a cell containing the figure you want to use as the top value.

> Number of divisions for Axis? (1-9)
> 37>View,2,Options,Scaling,Y-axis,B3,C2, ___

Careful here! The number of divisions does not include the base line, but it does include the top figure. So, if the range was from 0 to 100,000 and you wanted divisions every 10,000, then you would need to specify 10 divisions. That is not possible; 2,4,5 or 8 divisions here will give reasonable figures on the Y-axis, but any others will produce a mess of decimals.

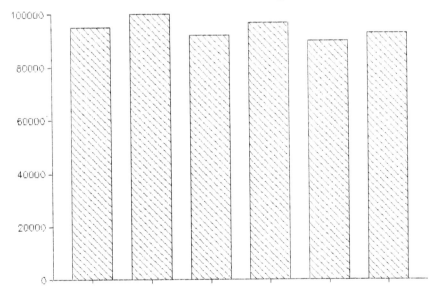

■ SECTION 30
Copying graphs

If you want to use the same basic graph with minor variations, then the specifications of graphs can be passed from one to another with the /**Copy** command. Use this sequence to copy Graph 1's details across to Graph 2:

/Copy,*,1,2

Similarly, you can Load in graph descriptions from one spreadsheet to use with another one:

/Load, **YEARSALE**, 1:4,2

This would copy the specifications of Graphs 1,2,3 and 4 from the Yearsale spreadsheet, into Graphs 2,3,4 and 5 of the current sheet. Where the sheets have the same layout and the same type and range of graphs are required in both, there is clearly a time-saving in this.

PART SIX

Financial applications

■ SECTION 31
The petty cash book

The task

To record the Receipts and Expenditure via Petty Cash, using analysis columns and keep typing to a minimum. Each entry needs to show the date and the nature of the transaction. Every item of expenditure must appear in the appropriate analysis column as well as in the main OUT column. Each month's records should be kept separately, with summaries transferred to an annual sheet.

The design

We could use a lookup table to reduce typing. This would require us to list every possible transaction and give it a code number. That would be feasible where only a limited number of different types were involved — stamps, petrol, stationery, and a few more. If there are a lot of possible types of entries, then a lookup table may well prove too unwieldy. It takes time to pull the table on screen in a window, and scan through it to find the code number of an entry. Far quicker to simply type it in!

On the other hand, some form of coding would be feasible for the analysis columns for you are unlikely to have more than a dozen of these at most. They can be recorded in a small, neat reference table, and as there are so few they will soon be remembered.

The basic layout of the monthly sheet is shown opposite. Each transaction will occupy a separate row — and in practice, you would probably need more than the 14 rows given here. The first five columns are the only ones in which Data will be entered. All transactions are recorded with dates in Column B and details in Column C; Receipts then go to the left and Expenditure to the right. All this is fairly standard for (paper) Petty Cash Books.

The analysis columns run from F to as far to the right as are needed — here they are limited to the four categories 'Motor', 'Post', 'Stationery' and 'Other'. The code numbers for these are shown at the top of the column. It is this code number that is entered in Column E.

The cells in the analysis columns all hold formulae that check the code in E, and copy the transaction value to their columns if the code is appropriate. For example, the formulae in F5 and G5 read:

```
F5                G5
IF(E5 = 1,D5,"#")   IF(E5 = 2,D5,"#")
```

Looking at the sample sheet, we can see that the 'Post' entry in Row 5 has put 12.50 in D5 and 2 in E5. When the formulae have done their

■ SECTION 31
The petty cash book

	A	B	C	D	E	F	G	H	I
1	PETTY CASH					1	2	3	4
2	Receipt	Date	Details	Total	Code	Motor	Post	Stat.	Other
3			Balance b/d	10.00					
4	50.00	1 Dec	Ex Cash a/c						
5		2	Post	12.50	2		12.50		
6		3	Cleaning	7.50	4				7.50
7		6	Petrol	13.00	1	13.00			
8		7	Post	8.00	2		8.00		
9		8	Stationery	3.75	3			3.75	
10		9	Oil	7.87	1	7.87			
11		10	Cleaning	7.50	4				7.50
12	50.00	13	Ex Cash a/c						
13		15	Ribbons	4.99	3			4.99	
14		16	Paint	7.99	4				7.99
15		17	Cleaning	7.50	4				7.50
16		18	Petrol	15.70	1	15.70			
17									
18									
19	100.00		Totals	96.30		36.57	20.50	8.74	30.49
20			Balance	13.70	MORE CASH				

work, F5 will show a space, but the 12.50 will have been copied into G5.

(If that space at the end of the formula seems a bit pointless to you, that is because it doesn't do anything at all. However, you cannot write a SuperCalc3 formula that says:

IF(E5 = 1,D5)

There must be a second value so that the formula can give some kind of result. Where you do not actually want a second value — as here — then use a zero or a space. Zeroes can produce nice neat columns of figures, but spaces make the active cells stand out better.

The bottom rows of the spreadsheet handle the totals and the running balance. The totals are all simple SUM expressions — it doesn't matter that much of the time they are adding cells with spaces in — they count as zero. The running balance in D20 is the product of the formula:

D3 + A19 − D19

This translates to mean 'Balance b/d + Total Receipts − Total

The petty cash book

Expenditure'. The level of the balance is checked by a formula in F20. If it falls below a minimum limit — here set at £15 — then a Prompt is displayed:

IF(D20<15,"MORE CASH"," ")

The sheet in use

An empty sheet is saved and kept as a permanent master copy. At the start of each month, this is loaded in and the month written in a prominent position — cell A1 being the best place. That copy of the sheet is saved under a new name, and used through the month. An eXecute file could simplify the daily loading and saving procedures.

At the end of each month, the figures from the Totals row are loaded (as a Part sheet) into the appropriate column of a simple annual record sheet. The month's sheet can then be left on the disk for future reference, and a printed output should be taken for the firm's records.

The annual sheet

This should have the same column structure as the monthly spreadsheet. In fact, the same master sheet can be used as a base, but the number of rows between the headings and the totals needs to be reduced to 12 — by /**Delete**. The formulae in the analysis columns are, of course, irrelevant here, but they are harmless and can be left.

Assuming that the monthly sheets have their totals on Row 30, and that the annual sheet takes its first month on Row 5, the January figures would be loaded in with a command like this:

Load,**JAN**,Part,**A30:M30,A5,V**alues

■ SECTION 32
Cashflow forecasts

The spreadsheet is an ideal tool for forecasting cashflows, for with a spreadsheet it is so easy to test out 'What if?' situations. What if sales can be increased by 5% over the year? What if our clients are slow payers? What if a payment is put off to another month? What if we invest in new machinery? When will it start to pay for itself, and how do we cover its costs? What if we take on this new building project? How much of an overdraft do we need to cover it, and how long do we need the overdraft facility?

You can ask these questions, and work out the answers without the use of a spreadsheet – but it takes so long. With a spreadsheet you can run through a whole range of possibilities in the time that it would take you to work out one with a pocket calculator.

A cashflow spreadsheet could be as simple as the home budget one developed earlier in the book. Its complexity depends upon the nature of the firm.

The sample cashflow shown on pages 128 and 129 is that of a small manufacturing firm. It sells approximately two-thirds of its output directly to the public, and the remainder to credit clients. Sales are seasonal, peaking in the summer months. The row headed **Credit Sales** represents estimated deliveries during the year – not the monies received for them. These are shown under **Debtors**. From past experience, it can be assumed that the majority of bills will be paid in the month after delivery, and this has been written into the spreadsheet. The formula used in most of that row has the shape:

90% of last month's sales + 10% from the month before

In cell D6, for example, this becomes:

90% C5 + 10% B5

(Cells B6 and C6 cannot use the formula as they would try to reference non-existent data. Their entries are estimated.)

The **Outgoings** are divided into Materials, Wages, Heat & Power, Rent & Rates and Motor Expenses. **Materials** vary directly with Sales, and represent 40% of the sales price. The firm knows that it must have its materials two months before the finished products are required, and that it will pay for them one month after receipt. Thus, the materials needed to meet the June Sales figures must be paid for in May. The materials formula takes these factors into account. For example, D11 holds this:

(E5 + E7) * .40)

	B ::	C ::	D ::	E ::	F ::	G ::	H ::	I ::	J ::	K ::	L ::	M ::	N ::
A	Jan	Feb	Mar	Apr	May	June	July	Aug	Sept	Oct	Nov	Dec	YEAR TOTALS
1:CASH FLOW													
2:Month													
3:BALANCE	2500	-1260	-1020	-2560	-2200	-2190	-2240	-1690	1560	4920	6130	5390	4550
4:INCOME													
5:Credit Sales	1000	2000	2000	2000	2000	3000	3000	2000	1000	1000	1000	500	20500
6:Debtors	500	900	1900	2000	2000	2000	2900	3000	2100	1100	1000	1000	20400
7:Cash Sales	1000	4000	2000	4000	4000	4000	4000	6000	6000	4000	2000	2000	43000
8:TOTAL IN	1500	4900	3900	6000	6000	6000	6900	9000	8100	5100	3000	3000	63400
9:													
10:OUTGOING													0
11:Materials	2400	1600	2400	2400	2800	2800	3200	2800	2000	1200	1000	800	25400
12:Wages	2400	2600	2600	2700	2700	2800	2700	2500	2300	2250	2200	2600	30350
13:Heat & Power	150	150	150	150	150	150	150	150	150	150	150	150	1800
14:Rent & Rates	250	250	250	250	250	250	250	250	250	250	250	250	3000
15:Motor Exp	60	60	40	140	90	50	50	50	40	40	140	40	800
16:													
17:TOTAL OUT	5260	4660	5440	5640	5990	6050	6350	5750	4740	3890	3740	3840	61350
18:													0
19:PROFIT/LOSS	-3760	240	-1540	360	10	-50	550	3250	3360	1210	-740	-840	2050
20:RUNNING BALANCE	-1260	-1020	-2560	-2200	-2190	-2240	-1690	1560	4920	6130	5390	4550	4550

	A	B	C	D	E	F	G	H	I	J	K	L	M	N
		Jan	Feb	Mar	Apr	May	June	July	Aug	Sept	Oct	Nov	Dec	YEAR TOTALS
1	CASH FLOW													
2	Month	Jan	Feb	Mar	Apr	May	June	July	Aug	Sept	Oct	Nov	Dec	
3	BALANCE	2500	240	80	-660	-200	210	460	1310	3760	5920	6280	5290	4550
4	INCOME													
5	Credit Sales	1000	2000	2000	2000	2000	3000	3000	2000	1000	1000	1000	500	20500
6	Debtors	600	1100	1900	2000	2000	2200	2900	2800	1900	1100	1000	900	20400
7	Cash Sales	1000	4000	2000	4000	4000	4000	4000	6000	6000	4000	2000	2000	43000
8	TOTAL IN	1600	5100	3900	6000	6000	6200	6900	8800	7900	5100	3000	2900	63400
9														
10	OUTGOING													0
11	Materials	800	2400	1600	2400	2400	2800	2800	3200	2800	2000	1200	1000	25400
12	Wages	2600	2400	2600	2600	2700	2700	2800	2700	2500	2300	2250	2200	30350
13	Heat & Power	150	150	150	150	150	150	150	150	150	150	150	150	1800
14	Rent & Rates	250	250	250	250	250	250	250	250	250	250	250	250	3000
15	Motor Exp	60	60	40	140	90	50	50	50	40	40	140	40	800
16														
17	TOTAL OUT	3860	5260	4640	5540	5590	5950	6050	6350	5740	4740	3990	3640	61350
18														
19	PROFIT/LOSS	-2260	-160	-740	460	410	250	850	2450	2160	360	-990	-740	2050
20	RUNNING BALANCE	240	80	-660	-200	210	460	1310	3760	5920	6280	5290	4550	4550

Wages also vary, though to a lesser extent. A combination of piece-work and basic wages means that the total rises with Sales. The additional wage costs are highest at the earlier stages of manufacturing, and lag two months behind sales. The formula to cover this relationship could be expressed as:

Base cost + 10% of sales two months ahead

It is also possible — and results in a shorter formula — to link them to material costs. As they lag one month behind sales, the formula takes the shape:

Base cost + 25% of next months material costs

In D12, for example, this produces:

2000 + 25% E11

The other costs are independent of Sales. The values entered there are based on known commitments and the previous year's figures.

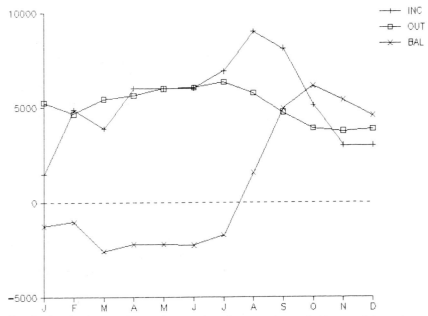

On the basis that a picture is worth a thousand words, his cashflow has been summarised in the graph shown above. Cast your eyes there, and

Cashflow forecasts

you will see that there are some cashflow problems facing this firm. Even with a starting balance of £2500, the firm is still overdrawn by over £2000 by the end of March — though it rises to a healthy £6750 in the late autumn.

The problems lie both in the seasonal nature of the trade, and the need to pay for raw materials and labour before the products are sold — some time before in the case of credit sales.

There are a number of possibilities that can be explored in the search for a more even cashflow — and reduced bank charges. If debtors could be encouraged to pay more promptly that might help. This can be tested quite readily. Let us assume that, by insisting that some bills — perhaps for small quantities — are paid in the month of delivery, 20% of credit sales are settled in the same month. The remainder would pay, as usual, one or two months in arrears. The formula to handle this would be (in D6):

20% D5 + 70% C5 + 10% B5

Once this formula is written in, and replicated across the row, the results will soon be visible. When the spreadsheet has been recalculated, the graph will show the new cash flow.

In practice, this particular change does not have a massive effect on the cashflow — it would be more significant if more customers could be persuaded to pay promptly. An alternative that could be explored is to delay payments for materials — assuming that it can be managed without causing problems with the suppliers. If the formula in the Materials row is rewritten so that the materials are paid for in the same month as the Sales to which they relate, it will look like this (in D11):

(D5 + D7) * .40

The result of these two alterations can be seen in the graph of the revised sheet shown overleaf.

The design

The main formulae used in this spreadsheet have been covered earlier, and they will not be directly applicable to many other firms. However, the principle of using the relationships between sales, income and costs to produce the figures for a cashflow is applicable. It is up to the firm to work out the links in their own situation and to write suitable formulae. The more accurately the relationships can be expressed, the more useful the final sheet will be, but even approximate percentage links will give a basis for a working forecast.

Cashflow forecasts

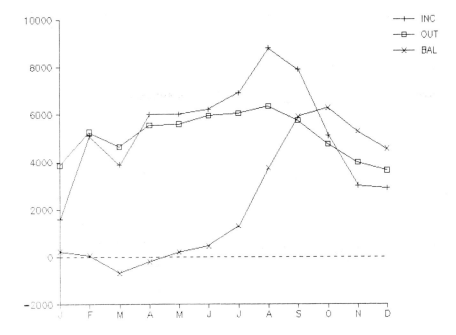

Income and Outgoings are all SUMmed down the columns and across the rows. Unless you are absolutely sure that you have covered all the categories in your initial layout, do remember to leave a blank row at the bottom of the Income and Outgoing rows for future expansion. The monthly **Profit/loss** figure is a simple **Income − Outgoings**.

The only thing to watch out for is the running balance. You will need to enter the starting balance at the top of the first column. The balance at the bottom is arrived at by **Start balance + Profit/loss**. This is then passed up to the top of the next column by giving the cell reference of the previous month's end balance. Here, for example, you will find **B20** written in cell **C4**.

Graphing will help to make things clearer. Select the Income, Outgoing and Balance rows as the data for the variables. A line graph will probably be easier to read than a bar chart.

While you are using the spreadsheet, it will be worth using a Title lock on the Headings column. This will keep them in view when you scroll to later months.

End-of-year accounts

Few small traders actively enjoy doing the end of the year accounts. They are a chore that have to be done, and anything that would make it easier should be welcome. This then is our aim here.

The task

To produce a spreadsheet that will draw up a Trial Balance, Profit and Loss Account and Final Balance sheet with no duplication of effort.

The design

The objective can be achieved by having a single **Data Entry** section, and drawing information from there for use in the analyses.

The relevant end-of-year figures will still have to be drawn from the accounts books or spreadsheets. They should be broken down as shown in the illustration below. The figures and the categories used here are from the accounts of an antique shop, but they should have a very much wider relevance.

	A		B		C		D		E	
1	BALANCES									
2	Data Entry									
3	Property		30000.00							
4	Capital		31736.56				Equip at start		2000.00	
5	Loans		.00				Purchases		2200.00	
6	Cash in bank		805.50				Depreciation		525.00	
7	Sales Income		72157.65							
8	Creditors		14197.35				EXPENSES			
9	Debtors		1035.86				Wages		15186.95	
10	Drawings		4900.00				Rent & Rates		1990.00	
11							Power		966.38	
12	Stock at start		16850.00				Advertising		796.37	
13	Purchases		40000.00				Bank Charges		.00	
14	Current Value		18500.00				Phone & Post		360.50	
15							Other		1000.00	

They have been grouped into four sections; finance and sales-related, stock, equipment and expenses. Additional or alternative categories of expenses may be appropriate. Working them into the design will create no problems as the expenses are grouped together throughout. If a 'Cash in Hand' entry is needed, this should be inserted next to the 'Cash in Bank' line, and the two added together. The single 'Cash' figure can then be used in later references.

Any other adjustments that may be needed in the design might be best left until after this example has been worked through.

Do make a note of any changes in layout, as the rest of the spreadsheet draws all of its data via references to cells in this section.

The **Trial Balance** includes all the items given in the Data Entry section, except **Current Stock Value** and **Depreciation of Equipment**.

The only items to go on the right-hand − **Credit** − side of the sheet are **Capital, Loans, Sales** and **Creditors**. All others are on the left. The SUMs at the bottom of each side should be the same. If they are not, first check that you have included all necessary items, then go over your figures again to see if any have been entered wrongly. If the two sides still fail to balance at this stage, you will need to return to your source figures and check through those.

```
         G         H          I        J
 1!TRIAL BALANCE    Dr.        Cr.
 2!Property        B3
 3!Capital                     B4
 4!Loans                       B5
 5!Bank c/acc.     B6
 6!Purchases       B13
 7!Stock at start  B12
 8!Drawings        B10
 9!Debtors         B9
10!Sales                       B7
11!Creditors                   B8
12!Equipment       E4+E5
13!Wages           E9
14!Rent & Rates    E10
15!Power           E11
16!Advertising     E12
17!Bank Charges    E13
18!Phone & Post    E14
19!Other           E15
20!                SUM(H2:H19) SUM(I2:I17)
```

End-of-year accounts

The Trading and Profit & Loss accounts

A standard layout is used here. At the top left, **Stock used** is calculated by the formula

Stock at start + Purchases − Stock at end

There are two more formulae just below. **Gross profit** is:

Sales − Stock used − Wages

The one immediately below is included as a check. This is traditional book-keeping and scarcely necessary here, where the calculations are always performed correctly − as long as they are given the right way! The result should be the same as the sales figure.

Stock used + Wages + Gross profit

The only other formula on the sheet finds the **Net profit** by subtracting the total expenses from the Gross profit. Notice how the SUM function is used inside the formula.

O11 − SUM(L12:L18)

```
          K      L      M          N       O
 1 TRADING & PROFIT & LOSS ACCOUNT
 2             Dr.                        Cr.
 3 Stock at Start B12          Sales        B7
 4 Purchase       B13
 5 Stock in Hand  B14
 6 Stock Used     L3+L4-L5
 7
 8 Wages          E9
 9 Gross Pr. c/d  O3-L6-L8
10 Check Sales    L6+L8+L9                  O3
11                            Gross Pr. b/d L9
12 Advertising    E12
13 Depreciation   E6
14 Rent & Rates   E10
15 Power          E11
16 Bank Charges   E13
17 Phone & Post   E14
18 Other          E15
19 Net Pr. c/d    O11-SUM(L12:L18)
20                            Net Pr. b/d   L19
```

End-of-year accounts

The Balance Sheet

A little more care is needed here with the cell references as values are drawn from both the Data Entry and the Profit & Loss Account sections.

Liabilities are summed in two stages. First the current Capital is reassessed:

Capital + Net Profit − Drawings

The result from this is then added to Loans and Creditors to give the **Total** at the bottom of the page.

Assets are the sum total of **Property, Cash, Debtors, Stock in hand** and **Equipment**. The figure for this last item is calculated from the Data Entry cells:

Equipment at start + Purchases − Depreciation

```
   !    Q    !!  R   !!   S   !!    T     !!  U   !!  V   !
 1 !BALANCE SHEET
 2 !            Liabilities              Assets
 3 !Capital     B4          Property     B3
 4 !+Net Profit O20         Cash in Bank B6
 5 !-Drawings   B10         Debtors      B9
 6 !Current Cap R3+R4-R5    Stock in hand B14
 7 !                        Equipment    E4+E5-E6
 8 !Loans       B5
 9 !Creditors   B8                       SUM(U3:U7)
10 !
11 !Total       R6+R8+R9
```

■ SECTION 34
Consolidation of spreadsheets

In Consolidation, values from a spreadsheet are added into a summary sheet, both having the same structure. It is often the most convenient way to produce quarterly or annual totals.

The example spreadsheet below is a simplified trading account summary, broken down by departments. Each month's figures are entered on a blank copy of the master spreadsheet, and Saved separately for future reference.

	A	B	C	D	E	F
1	CONSOLIDATION					
2	January					
3		Dept.1	Dept. 2	Dept. 3	Dept.4	Total
4						
5	Sales	2300	2500	2000	2800	SUM(B5:E5)
6	Purchases	1250	1400	900	1500	SUM(B6:E6)
7	Wages	900	750	800	900	SUM(B7:E7)
8	Gross Profit	B5-B6-B7	C5-C6-C7	D5-D6-D7	E5-E6-E7	F5-F6-F7
9						
10	Expenses	200	150	250	200	SUM(B10:E10)
11						
12	Profit	B8-B10	C8-C10	D8-D10	E8-E10	F8-F10

The annual summary sheet can then be Loaded in on top of the completed monthly sheet, using the **Consolidate** option.

Load,**ANNUAL,C**onsolidate

Values in corresponding cells are summed together as the second sheet is Loaded. New formulae will replace existing ones — though this will be irrelevant where both are the same. Where the new sheet has different or additional text this will overwrite anything beneath.

The resulting sheet is then Saved, and put aside until the end of the next month.

Save,**ANNUAL,B**ackup,**A**ll

■ SECTION 34
Consolidation of spreadsheets

	A	B	C	D	E	F
1	CONSOLIDATION					
2	Summary Sheet					
3		Dept.1	Dept. 2	Dept. 3	Dept.4	Total
4						
5	Sales	7900	8700	7350	8300	32250
6	Purchases	4300	4600	3400	4450	16750
7	Wages	2700	2250	2400	2700	10050
8	Gross Profit	900	1850	1550	1150	5450
9						
10	Expenses	850	450	725	600	2625
11						
12	Profit	50	1400	825	550	2825
13						
14	Or Load Part Only and SUM as needed					
15						
16	Jan	-50	200	50	200	400
17	Feb	0	300	450	200	950
18	March	100	900	325	150	1475
19						0
20	Total	50	1400	825	550	2825

Partial Consolidation

There is always a danger with computer use that too much data is retained. Some people would argue that you can never have too much information about your business, but it is quite possible to get bogged down in detail. For a start, the more disks you have, and the more files you have on each disk, the longer it takes to track down the one you want. Likewise, the more information that is present in a spreadsheet, the longer it takes to focus on the parts that are relevant to the task in hand. Therefore, it is a good idea to winnow your data at each stage of the processing.

If the purpose of the annual summary is to give an overview of the performance of the departments, then the spreadsheet for this need not be much more complex than that shown above. On the other hand, the monthly sheets may need to carry a greater degree of detail. The figures for the various categories of Sales, Purchases and Expenses must be brought together somewhere along the line. What is needed then, at the end of each month, is a means of drawing the summarised data out of the detailed sheet.

■ SECTION 34
Consolidation of spreadsheets

This can be done by creating a summary area on a part of the monthly sheet. Sub-totals from the main part of the sheet can be transferred down to it automatically by cell references, so that no work is needed to maintain the summaries. At the end of the month, this summary area can be loaded into the annual sheet. The only requirement is that the cell layout must correspond. If, for example, the monthly sheet had a part structured as shown above, but sited at A51 to F75, it could be brought into the annual sheet in this way. First, the annual sheet would need to be loaded, then part of the monthly sheet added into it with this command:

Load,**JAN**,Part,**A51:F75,A1**, +

The **Part** load will take in only the specified section of the sheet, and will Load it on top of the existing sheet. The + sign at the end asks SuperCalc3 to consolidate the corresponding cells.

Alternative summaries

It may be that you need to keep some aspects of the monthly figures separate on the annual summary sheet. A Part Load can be the answer here too. You can see this in the second of the two illustrations at the beginning of this section, where the **Profit** row for each month is brought into the summary, and used to keep a running check on the performance of each department.

The end of the month housekeeping for March − using the sheet layout as shown here − would then go through these stages.

1   Load a blank master copy of the monthly sheet:
    Load,**MASTER**,All

2   Fill in figures and Save.
    Save,**MARCH**,All

3   Clear the sheet and Load in the annual summary.
    Zap,Yes
    Load,**ANNUAL**,All

4   Add in the latest figures with a simple consolidation.
    Load,**MARCH**,Consolidate

5   Pull in the March Profit line.
    Load,**MARCH**,Part,**B13:F13,B19**

6   Save the update summary.
    Save,**ANNUAL**,All

■ SECTION 35
The VAT return

With so many different schemes currently used for calculating the VAT Return, it is not possible to include all of them here, but the main features of the spreadsheets needed should be visible in the examples given.

The task

The purpose of this spreadsheet is rather like that of the End-of-the-Year Accounts sheet one that was developed in Section 33. For the most part it is used to pull together information that has been produced by other spreadsheets or manual methods, though some calculations are involved.

The design

The sheet is divided into two sections. Data is collected, mainly in the top half of the sheet, then collated and presented in the standard VAT Return format in the bottom right corner.

This particular sheet may be more complicated than is needed for your own purposes, as this caters for three different VAT schemes − A, B and H. Those traders, especially retailers, who use a combination of two or more schemes may find that a very similar sheet is necessary.

The VAT schemes

Scheme A is the simplest to operate. It is used where all Outputs (Sales) are at Standard Rate. The sole figure needed here is for Daily Gross Takings including VAT. In this sheet, the value is entered in E6, then copied from there into G6, as the Taxable amounts are collected into that column.

Scheme B is for those retailers with Outputs at both Standard and Zero Rates. It requires the user to work out the total retail value of new stock acquired during the VAT period. The Taxable Output is based on the formula:

Taxable output = Daily gross takings − New zero-rated stock

Scheme H is similar to Scheme B, but here a Standard-rated fraction is found by comparing the standard-rated new stock with the total new stock, both figures being at cost price and including VAT where applicable. The Daily gross takings are then multiplied by that fraction to produce the Taxable output.

The formulae used in this section of the spreadsheet are worth a closer look. The Standard-rated fraction is arrived at by simple division in cell E18. If this part of the sheet is not used, so that the values in E16 and E17

■ SECTION 35
The VAT return

```
   !  A   ::   B   ::   C   ::   D   ::   E   ::   F   ::   G   ::   H   ::
 1 !VAT RETURN
 2 !
 3 !CALCULATION OF TAXABLE OUTPUT          DATA HERE          TAXABLE
 4 !
 5 !Scheme A - all outputs at standard
 6 !Daily Gross Takings Inc. VAT........ 0              E6
 7 !
 8 !STOCK VALUES AT SELLING PRICE,INC.VAT
 9 !
10 !Scheme B  - outputs at both rates
11 !Daily Gross Takings Inc. VAT........ 0
12 !Zero-rated new stock.............. 0              E11-E12
13 !
14 !Scheme H - outputs at both rates
15 !Daily Gross Takings Inc. VAT........ 30000
16 !Standard rated new stock.......... 18000
17 !Total new stock this period....... 27000
18 !Standard rated Fraction          E16/E17          IF(NOT(ISERROR(E18)),
                                                      E15*E18,0)
19 !
20 !D.G.T.    E6+E11+E15        TAXABLE OUTPUTS    G6+G12+G18
21 !
22 !COLLATION OF FIGURES
23 !
24 !VAT RATE  15
25 !VAT FRACT B24/(100+B24)
26 !                               OUTPUT TAX........ G20*B25
27 !                               Underdeclarations  0
28 !                               VAT DUE........... H26+H27
29 !Taxed Inputs inc. Vat..... 13800
30 !Inputs at zero rate....... 7000
31 !Total Inputs.............. D29+D30   INPUT TAX       D29*B25
32 !                               Overdeclarations   0
33 !                               VAT DEDUCTIBLE    H31+H32
34 !
35 !                               NET VAT   IF(H35<0 H28-H33
36 !
37 !                               Value of Outputs   B20-H26
38 !                               Value of Inputs    D31-H31
```

were zero, then the formula would produce an **ERROR** display, and any other formulae which referenced that cell would also show ERROR. It is therefore necessary to include a check for this in the next calculation. G18 contains the formula to calculate the Taxable output. It is essentially

Daily gross takings * Standard-rated fraction

but the possibility of ERROR means that the formula actually used in G18 looks like this:

IF(ISERROR(E18),0,E15 * E18)

This checks for an **ERROR** result in E18, and if it finds one it will place a zero in G18; otherwise it will work out the Taxable output as normal.

(The functions **ISNUM, ISDATE, ISTEXT** and **ISNA** can be used in the same fashion to see if a cell contains a NUMber, DATE, TEXT or NA (Not Applicable) entry.)

Input data

No matter what VAT scheme is used, the Input data need to be collected in the same way. There are two entries − the totals of all Zero- and Standard-rated inputs (stock and expenses) for the period including VAT.

The VAT Fraction

This could be entered directly as 3/23, using the form advised by HM Customs and Excise, or it can be calculated from the current VAT Rate. The latter method is used in the example sheet. With the rate entered in B24, the fraction is calculated by the formula:

B24/(100 + B24)

The result is the same, as the formula produces 15/115, which cancels down to 3/23. However, if the VAT rate changes, the new figure can be entered into B24 without having to work out the new fraction or wait for the VATman to tell you it.

The VAT return

Collation of figures

The layout of this section has been designed to match the VAT Return form. It may be possible, depending on your printer, to use it to print the entries directly onto the form, though a manual transfer may well be simpler.

Output tax is calculated by multiplying the Taxable output by the VAT fraction. Underdeclarations, if any, are added in to give the final VAT DUE figure.

Similarly, **Input tax** is the product of Taxable inputs and the VAT fraction. It is added to any Overdeclarations to give the VAT result.

The **Net VAT** line contains this formula which checks the Net VAT figure (in H35) to give you a reminder:

IF(H35<0,"REPAYABLE","PAYABLE")

Finally, the **Value of outputs** and **inputs** are arrived at by deducting the VAT figures from the Daily gross takings and Total inputs.

■ SECTION 36
Loans

In this section we will develop a number of small modules, each concerned with a different aspect of interest calculations. They have been written separately here, for clarity, but you may wish to combine some or all of them into one Loan utility spreadsheet, or work them into other accounting sheets.

Credit card costs

How much does it cost to borrow money with a credit card? When interest rates are quoted on a monthly basis, they can be deceptive — as many borrowers have found. Interest is calculated daily on the amount owing, so that the current 2% a month rate is actually equivalent to almost 27% a year — nearly twice the current overdraft rate.

The precise cost of a Barclaycard-style loan, and its APR (Annualised Percentage Rate) can be worked out with the formulae shown in the following:

```
 :  A  ::  B  ::  C  ::  D  ::    E      ::  F  :: G :
1:LOANS
2:Barclaycard style. Interest quoted by month, calculated by day.
3:Amount    50
4:Int.Rate  2
5:          Day     Month   Year    Date
6:From      11      11      86      DATE(C6,B6,D6)   JDATE(E6)
7:To        9       2       87      DATE(C7,B7,D7)   JDATE(E7)
8:                                  Days .......... F7-F6
9:Cost      B3*(1+B4/100)^(F8/30)-B3
10:Annual Rate        100*(1+B4/100)^(12)-100
```

For the calculations to be made, the spreadsheet needs to know the timespan of the loan as well as the amount and monthly interest rate. The timespan in **Days** is worked out from the start and end dates using two of SuperCalc3's functions — DATE and JDATE.

DATE needs the figures for month, day and year. These may be given directly, e.g. **5,4,87** or via cell references — as happens here. It does not merely display the figures in a neat format, it also checks them, and recalculates if necessary. Thus if you gave it '2' for the month and '30' for the days, it would display the date (this year) as '3/2/1987' or (next year) as '3/1/1988'.

JDATE takes a DATE value and converts it into the number of days since 1 March 1900 — the startpoint of the Modified Julian Calendar. By itself

Loans

this is not terribly useful, but by finding the JDATE value of two dates, you can easily work out the number of days that have elapsed.

In the example shown below, the dates 11/11/1986 and 2/9/1987 are converted into the values 31667 and 31757 by the JDATE functions in column F. The difference between them is shown in F8.

```
    !  A   !!  B   !!  C   !!  D   !!     E     !!  F  !! G !
 1!LOANS
 2!Barclaycard style. Interest quoted by month, calculated by day.
 3!Amount      50.00
 4!Int.Rate      2
 5!        Day     Month    Year    Date
 6!From     11      11       86     11/11/1986     31667
 7!To        9       2       87      2/ 9/1987     31757
 8!                                 Days .......... 90
 9!Cost    3.06
10!Annual Rate      26.82
```

The **Cost** and **Annual rate** of the loan are calculated using variations on the standard compound interest formula. This normally takes the form:

CAPITAL * (1 + I.R.) ^ TIME

where IR is the Interest rate, as a decimal fraction, and TIME is the period of the loan. The way that it works can be seen in this simple example.

Take a capital amount of £100 and an interest rate of 10% a year over a period of three years. The growth of the capital can be seen in this sequence.

	Capital	Interest @ 10%	End-of-year capital
Year 1	£100.00	£10.00	£110.00
Year 2	£110.00	£11.00	£121.00
Year 3	£121.00	£12.10	£133.10

Put the same figure into the formula and you get:

£100 * (1 + .10) ^ 3 = £100 * 1.1 ^ 3 = £100 * 1.331 = £133.10

The APR calculation uses the formula, finding the interest on £100 over 12 months:

100 * (1 + B4/100) ^ 12 − 100

(The £100 is taken away at the end so that only the interest is left.)

Loans

Further adjustment is needed in the Cost formula. The period of the loan is measured in days and must be converted to months. The expression (Days/30) is sufficiently accurate for most purposes.

The final shape of this formula is therefore:

CAPITAL * (1 + I.R) ^ (DAYS/30) − CAPITAL

or

B3 * (1 + B4/100) ^ (F8/30) − B3

Overdrafts

The formulae used here are virtually the same as in those for the credit card calculations. The only real changes are in the time period parts of **Cost** and **Annual rate**.

```
  ¦  A   ¦¦  B   ¦¦  C   ¦¦  D   ¦¦      E      ¦¦   F   ¦
1¦LOANS
2¦Overdraft - here using averaged overdraft
3¦Av. OD    200
4¦Int. Rate 15
5¦         Day     Month   Year    Date
6¦From     1       2       87      DATE(C6,B6,D6)  JDATE(E6)
7¦To       11      11      87      DATE(C7,B7,D7)  JDATE(E7)
8¦                                 Days            F7-F6
9¦Cost     B3*(1+B4/100)^(F8/365)-B3
```

Overdrafts are calculated daily on an annual rate. The DAYS must therefore be converted to fractions of years with the expression **DAYS/365**:

B3 * (1 + B4/100) ^ (F8/365) − B3

The **Annual rate** calculation is scarcely necessary, as overdraft interest rates are quoted on that basis. This adaptation of the formula used in the credit card module merely proves that the interest rate is the APR:

100 * (1 + B4/100) − 100

■ SECTION 36
Loans

Structured loans

With these, the interest is charged on the initial amount of the loan throughout the period of the loan — even though the actual amount owed is decreasing steadily as payments are made. The quoted interest rate is normally several percent below the normal overdraft rate, but the APR will prove to be substantially higher. The formulae are rather different in this module.

```
     !  A  !!  B  !!  C  !!  D  !!    E    !
 1 !LOANS
 2 !Structured Loan - Interest payable on all capital
 3 !Interest at annual rate
 4 !Amount          200
 5 !Int. Rate       10
 6 !Annual Interest C5%C4
 7 !Term in months  24
 8 !Term in Years   C7/12
 9 !Total Interest  C5%C4*C7/12
10 !Total Cost      C4+C9
11 !Monthly Outlay  C10/C7
12 !Monthly Repayment C4/C7
13 !Equivalent Loan (C4+C12)/2
14 !A.P.R.          (C6/C13)*100
```

Time periods are much easier to handle as they are almost always over a fixed term, and measured in months.

Total interest is the product of Capital, Interest rate and number of years. The percentage function may be convenient here:

C5% C4 * C7/12   (I.R. % of Amount * Months/12)

Total cost adds the Interest to the Capital, and **Monthly outlay** divides this by the term.

The remaining formulae are all concerned with calculating the APR. They revolve around the need to find a single figure to express the amount that is borrowed — when this sum is changing every month. Take a simple example.

Loans

Suppose you borrowed £50 for five months (interest free!) and paid it back at £10 per month. Your debt would be:

Month 1   £50
Month 2   £40
Month 3   £30
Month 4   £20
Month 5   £10

You could look at this another way. You have borrowed £10 for 1 month, £10 for 2 months, £10 for 3 months, £10 for 4 months and another £10 for 5 months. It is the same as borrowing £10 for 1 + 2 + 3 + 4 + 5 (= 15) months, or £150 for 1 month or £30 (the central figure) for the original 5-month term. Here then is the single figure that we need.

```
      :  A  ::  B  ::  C  ::  D  ::    E    :
 1 :LOANS
 2 :Structured Loan - Interest payable on all capital
 3 :Interest at annual rate
 4 :Amount              200.00
 5 :Int. Rate            10.00
 6 :Annual Interest      20
 7 :Term in months       24
 8 :Term in Years         2
 9 :Total Interest       40.00
10 :Total Cost          240.00
11 :Monthly Outlay       10.00
12 :Monthly Repayment     8.33
13 :Equivalent Loan     104.17
14 :A.P.R.               19.20
```

Let's work through those final formulae. The **Monthly repayment** is the capital divided by the number of months in the original term. In the example above, this is £200/24 or £8.33. If we add that to the initial amount and halve it, we will get the value of the **Equivalent loan**.

(C4 + C12)/2

Now take the Annual interest, divide this by the Equivalent loan, and you have the Interest rate. Multiply it by 100 to give a percentage figure:

APR = (C6/C13)*100

The £200 structured loan at 10% over 24 months was equivalent to borrowing £104.17 at 19.20%.

■ SECTION 36
Loans

Mortgages

There are two quick ways to work out the repayments on a mortgage, and both are shown in the illustration below.

```
     :      A      ::   B   :: C ::     D      ::    E    ::  F  :
 1 :MORTGAGE
 2 :
 3 :Mortgage Value    40000         Tax Free Portion IF(B3>=B11,B11,B3)
 4 :Interest Rate %   12.25         Interest         B4%E3
 5 :Interest Rate     B4/100        Less Tax         B10%E4
 6 :Term of Years     25            Per Month        E5/12
 7 :Annual Repayment  (B3*B5)/(1-1/(1+B5)^B6)
 8 :Monthly Repayment B7/12         Net Monthly Cost B8-E6
 9 :                                                 ------------
10 :Tax Rate %        29
11 :Tax Relief limit  30000
12 :
13 :-------------------------------------------------------------
14 :Using PMT function
15 :
16 :Mortgage value    B3
17 :Monthly Int. Rate B5/12
18 :Term of Months    B6*12
19 :PMT(B17,B18,B19)  PMT(B16,B17,B18)
20 :
```

The first method uses this formula:

$$\frac{\text{Capital} \times \text{Interest rate}}{1 - [1/(1 + \text{Interest rate})^{\text{Time}}]}$$

Anyone with an interest in mathematics may be tempted to explore it to see how it works. The rest of us may simply accept that it does! As a SuperCalc3 formula it looks like this:

(B3 * B5)/(1 − 1/(1 + B5) ^ B6)

The formula converts this to a monthly repayment, ignoring tax relief. That is calculated on the right-hand side. The only formula there of any complexity is the one that finds the amount that is subject to tax relief.

IF(B3> = B11,B11,B3)

If the mortgage is above the limit, then the ceiling value will result from this, otherwise the whole amount will be given.

It should be noted that this section will only give an accurate figure for the first year of the mortgage, or for as long as the amount owing is more than the tax-relief limit. The tax-relief is only on the interest on the mortgage, not on the repayments. As the principal is slowly paid off, so the interest declines. The second method of calculating mortgage repayments uses SuperCalc3's **PMT** function. This takes the capital, the interest rate, and the number of periods. The form is always:

    PMT(amount,int.rate,periods)

Give it an annual interest rate and number of years, and you will get an annual repayment figure. Here, monthly figures are used instead:

```
   !      A     !!   B    !! C !!    D       !!    E    !! F !
 1 !MORTGAGE
 2 !
 3 !Mortgage Value    40000.00    Tax Free Portion   30000.00
 4 !Interest Rate %      12.25    Interest            3675.00
 5 !Interest Rate        .1225    Less Tax            1065.75
 6 !Term of Years        25.00    Per Month             88.81
 7 !Annual Repayment   5188.67
 8 !Monthly Repayment   432.39    Net Monthly Cost     343.58
 9 !
10 !Tax Rate %           29.00
11 !Tax Relief limit  30000.00
12 !
13 !----------------------------------------------------------
14 !Using PMT function
15 !
16 !Mortgage value    40000.00
17 !Monthly Int. Rate     .0102
18 !Term of Months      300.00
19 !PMT(B17,B18,B19)    428.70
20 !
```

As you will see in the example above, the PMT function gives a slightly more cheerful result, but the variation is no more than you would find by approaching two different building societies.

■ SECTION 37
Investments

The PMT function, and the loan calculations covered in the last section could be used to find the returns on investments as long as that return can be expressed in terms of an interest rate.

SuperCalc3 has four other functions that are specifically designed for analysing investments on the basis of cashflows. They are **NPV, PV, IRR** and **FV**.

NPV (Net Present Value) and **PV** (Present Value) are demonstrated in the illustration below. They are both concerned with the effective return on an investment after discounting for cost of capital. An allowance for inflation may also be written into the discount rate.

	A		B		C		D		E		F	
1	PRESENT VALUE								IRR BY GRAPH			
2												
3	Capital	25000.00			Year	Discounted return	GRAPH DATA				
4	Returns	6000.00			1	5454.55		.01	increment	
5		5500.00			2	4545.45				
6		5500.00			3	4132.23		.10	5413.07	
7		5000.00			4	3415.07		.11	4257.19	
8		5000.00			5	3104.61		.12	3171.52	
9		4500.00			6	2540.13		.13	2150.65	
10		4500.00			7	2309.21		.14	1189.70	
11		4000.00			8	1866.03		.15	284.16	
12		4000.00			9	1696.39		.16	-570.02	
13		3500.00			10	1349.40		.17	-1376.60	
14	Total	47500.00			Total	30413.07		.18	-2138.97	
15	NPV	5413.07			– Capital	5413.07		.19	-2860.27	
16								.20	-3543.36	
17								.21	-4190.85	
18	Present Value on fixed returns									
19	PV(5000,.1,10)			30722.84						
20										

NPV is used where the anticipated income will vary over time. It needs to be given the discount rate and the range of values expected – in the example shown here, the rate was written into the formula as .1, or 10%, and the anticipated returns over a ten-year period are listed from B4 to B13. This gives:

NPV(.10,B4:B13)

Investments

The capital outlay must be deducted from that to produce the true Net Present Value figure. The expression in B15 is:

NPV(.10,B4:B13)-B3

and it displays £5413.07.

The calculations in column D produce the same results the long way — simply to show how NPV works. The anticipated returns in column B are discounted by 10% raised to the power of the number of years. Thus, for example, in Row 8 you will see that with a discount rate of 10%, a return of £5000 in 5 years time will be worth £3104.61 at today's values. The total of these discounted returns, minus the initial investment gives the same result as the NPV function.

PV is used where the returns will be at a constant level. The function needs the return, the discount rate and the number of years (or months if the discount rate is monthly). It produces the sum of the discounted returns, so that the example

PV(5000,.1,10)

results in £30722.84. You could have got the same result by using NPV on a range of cells all containing 5000.

The **IRR** (Internal Rate of Return) function is designed to tell you the discount rate at which the effective return on an investment would be zero. In theory you simply give it the range of cells containing the returns, and (optionally) a guessed discount rate; it should then compute the correct value. In practice, this particular function does not seem to have been implemented properly on the current version of SuperCalc3. It is very difficult to get anything other than an ERROR message from it.

If you do need to calculate the IRR of an investment, it can be done as shown in columns E and F:

Column E contains a range of discount rates. By altering the start value, and the **increment**, the range can be changed. The formulae in column F all perform an NVP function on the range of values in B4:B13, but with the discount rate from the corresponding row in the E column.

If the results in F6:F17 are turned into a Line Graph, the IRR point will be clearly visible, as you can see here:

Investments

```
 !   A   !!   B   !!   C   !!      D        !!  E  !!       F          !
1!PRESENT VALUE                               IRR BY GRAPH
2!
3!  Capital    25000    Year Discounted return GRAPH DATA
4!  Returns     6000      1   B4*(1/1.1)^C4     .01            increment
5!             5500     C4+1  B5*(1/1.1)^C5
6!             5500     C5+1  B6*(1/1.1)^C6     .1    NPV(E6,B4:B13)-B3
7!             5000     C6+1  B7*(1/1.1)^C7    E6+E4  NPV(E7,B4:B13)-B3
8!             5000     C7+1  B8*(1/1.1)^C8    E7+E4  NPV(E8,B4:B13)-B3
9!             4500     C8+1  B9*(1/1.1)^C9    E8+E4  NPV(E9,B4:B13)-B3
10!            4500     C9+1  B10*(1/1.1)^C10  E9+E4  NPV(E10,B4:B13)-B3
11!            4000    C10+1  B11*(1/1.1)^C11  E10+E4 NPV(E11,B4:B13)-B3
12!            4000    C11+1  B12*(1/1.1)^C12  E11+E4 NPV(E12,B4:B13)-B3
13!            3500    C12+1  B13*(1/1.1)^C13  E12+E4 NPV(E13,B4:B13)-B3
14!  TotalM(B4:B13)     Total  SUM(D4:D13)     E13+E4 NPV(E14,B4:B13)-B3
15!   NPV4:B13)-B3 - Capital         D14-B3    E14+E4 NPV(E15,B4:B13)-B3
16!                                            E15+E4 NPV(E16,B4:B13)-B3
17!                                            E16+E4 NPV(E17,B4:B13)-B3
18!Present Value on fixed returns
19!PV(5000,.1,10)        PV(5000,.1,10)
```

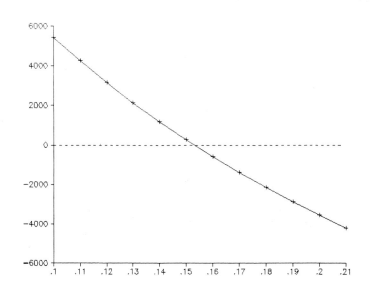

Investments

FV calculates the future value of a regular investment at a fixed rate of interest over a number of years. There is a slight oddity to it, in that the result will include the investment for the final year, but not the interest. You can see this in the figure below, where the FV function is shown alongside a table that calculates the growing savings. The expression:

FV(1000,.1,10)

gives a value of £15937.42. You will find the same figure at the bottom of column D, where it represents the accumulated capital and interest from the end of year 9, plus an additional £1000. If you wanted to use FV to find the position at the end of Year 10, then you would need to write it this way:

FV(1000,.1,11)-1000

	A	B	C	D	E	F
1	Future Value					
2						
3			Year	Capital	Interest	End of Year
4	Payment	1000.00	1.00	1000.00	100.00	1100.00
5	Int. Rate	.10	2.00	2100.00	210.00	2310.00
6	Periods	10.00	3.00	3310.00	331.00	3641.00
7			4.00	4641.00	464.10	5105.10
8			5.00	6105.10	610.51	6715.61
9			6.00	7715.61	771.56	8487.17
10			7.00	9487.17	948.72	10435.89
11			8.00	11435.89	1143.59	12579.48
12			9.00	13579.48	1357.95	14937.42
13			10.00	15937.42	1593.74	17531.17
14	fv(b4,b5,b6)	15937.42			5937.42	
15	10*10000+9 Years Interest					

■ SECTION 38
Cost accounting

A manufacturing firm that produces different lines will find it useful to find the cost of production of those lines, and hence their relative profitability. If it is feasible to concentrate on more profitable lines then the overall trading position of the firm can be improved. Such a concentration is not, of course, always possible. It may be that the market for the most profitable goods is limited, or the less profitable ones are an essential part of the range of goods produced. There may be other constraints on the use of resources within the firm. Nevertheless, better business decisions will be made if the relative costs of production are known.

	A	B	C	D	E
1:COST ACCOUNTING	Car Stereo	Personal	Midi System	Total	
2:Opening Stock	60000.00	80000.00	10000.00	150000.00	
3:+ Purchases	440000.00	530000.00	250000.00	1220000.00	
4:- Closing Stock	60000.00	70000.00	15000.00	145000.00	
5:STOCK USED	440000.00	540000.00	245000.00	1225000.00	
6:					
7:Wages	200000.00	350000.00	30000.00	580000.00	
8:PRIME COST	640000.00	890000.00	275000.00	1805000.00	
9:					
10:Fuel & Power	13000.00	13000.00	13000.00	39000.00	
11:Depreciation	47000.00	90000.00	30000.00	167000.00	
12:FACTORY COST	700000.00	993000.00	318000.00	2011000.00	
13:					
14:Sales Numbers	8000	20000	1000	29000	
15:Unit Sales Price	99.75	51.50	375.00		
16:PRIME UNIT COST	80.00	44.50	275.00		
17:FACTORY UNIT COST	87.50	49.65	318.00		
18:UNIT PROFIT	12.25	1.85	57.00		
19:					
20:PROFIT ON COST %	14.00%	3.73%	17.92%		

The illustration above shows the spreadsheet for a cost analysis of a small hifi company. Those rows with headings in capitals contain calculated figures. The rest are supplied by the user. The formulae given in this explanation are all from column B.

The **PRIME COST** (B5 + B7) is the sum of the total **STOCK USED** (B2 + B3-B4) and **Wages**. This is later divided by **Sales numbers** to produce the **PRIME UNIT COST**.

The **FACTORY COST** (B8 + B10 + B11) takes overheads into account. You will note that **Fuel & power** values are the same throughout the example, as it is assumed that these costs cannot be meaningfully split between the separate production lines. On the other hand, **Depreciation** does vary, because the cost of the items of machinery can be assessed separately.

The **UNIT PROFIT** (B15-B17) represents the difference between the **Sales price** and **FACTORY UNIT COST**. If this is divided by the Cost (B18/B17), it gives the **PROFIT ON COST %**. This has been converted into a percentage figure on screen by selecting a user-defined Format in which the **%** flag was switched on.

The bottom line of the sheet then shows clearly the relative profitability of the firm's products. In this particular example, the management should now be performing a break-even analysis to find a better price/sales level balance (or contemplating getting out of the personal stereo market!).

Forecasting

One of the advantages of performing this kind of cost analysis is that it allows you to forecast future cost more accurately. The sheet can be extended to include columns in which the percentage changes over the year are written, and the resulting values calculated.

The formula for raising a value by a given percentage may by either:

VALUE + PERCENTAGE % VALUE   (using the **%** function)

or

VALUE * (1 + PERCENTAGE/100)

PART SEVEN

Statistics and the spreadsheet

Totals and averages

The term 'Statistics' covers a wide variety of techniques and practices all of which are intended to draw meaning out of masses of numbers; to show underlying trends and give pointers to the future; to reveal the relationships − if any − between events.

The more visible aspects of Supercalc3 statistics − Graphs − have been covered earlier. Here we will look at some of the numerical techniques.

Collection and collation of data

All statistical work starts with the observation and collection of data, and exactly how this is managed depends upon the nature of what is being recorded.

With **discrete variables** every item will fall into a distinct category. Off-the-rack women's clothes, for example, will be of a particular size − 10, 12, 14 or whatever. Someone monitoring the sales from a clothes shop might then produce a table like this:

Size	8	10	12	14	16
No. sold	23	35	58	52	24

Continuous variables are those where the quantities are measured, and sizes or weights merge imperceptibly from one to the next. If the sales manager monitoring the sales of clothes had also recorded the heights of the customers, the table would have had to take a different form. People do not slot into set sizes and it is of little value to have a long string of measurements, individually recorded. Instead, you have to take a decision about how you want to group the measurements. Here it might be useful to collect the heights into 2-inch groups:

Height	Under 5'	−5'2"	−5'4"	−5'6"	over 5'6"
No.	25	27	50	64	16

It may often be easier to group your statistics in this way before turning to the spreadsheet for the analysis, but sometimes the data will be supplied in 'raw' form. In this event, the figures can be collated by the sheet.

The figure below shows how a set of raw data − the values in column B − can be sorted into the groups $0-5$, $6-10$, $11-15$ and $16+$. Glance down column C and you will notice a '1' for every value that is between 0 and 5.

■ SECTION 39
Totals and averages

The formulae in this block are all essentially the same. That in cell C3 reads:

IF(AND(B3> = 0,B3< = 5),1,0)

The expression **AND(B3> = 0,B3< = 5)** tests B3 against both of the limits for the group. **AND** should be used wherever you need to test two conditions, and where both must be true.

	A	B	C	D	E	F
1	AVERAGES					
2		Number	0-5	6-10	11-15	16+
3		12.5	0	0	1	0
4		3	1	0	0	0
5		10.3	0	0	1	0
6		4	1	0	0	0
7		14.7	0	0	1	0
8		15.9	0	0	0	1
9		8.8	0	1	0	0
10		13	0	0	1	0
11		3.3	1	0	0	0
12		7.2	0	1	0	0
13		9.9	0	1	0	0
14		5.3	0	1	0	0
15		16	0	0	0	1
16		19.4	0	0	0	1
17		12.3	0	0	1	0
18		--				
19	Totals	155.6	3	4	5	3
20	Mean =	12.96667				

The number of '1's in each groups column can be found by using a simple SUM. If the checking formulae are altered so that they produce a '1' or a blank cell rather than '1' or '0', then the statistical function **COUNT** may be used instead.

COUNT(C3:C14)

will give the number of cells in that range that contain a value. As '0' is a valid number in statistics, the cells must be blank if they are not to be counted.

■ SECTION 39
Totals and averages

Though only a very few numbers are involved here, the same method can be used on a much wider scale to handle more realistic quantities of data.

Averages

There are three different types of average in statistical terms. The **Mean**, or arithmetic average, is produced by dividing the total of a set of numbers by their count. It is perhaps the most commonly used type of average, but can be misleading in some situations. Take, for instance, a small firm where the boss pays himself £1000 a week, and pays his five workers £100 each. Is it meaningful to say that the average wage in that firm is £250?

With SuperCalc3, you can find the average of a set either by SUMming the numbers and dividing by the COUNT; or by using the function **AV(range)**. This will calculate the mean directly.

The **Mode** is the most common value. With SuperCalc3, the easiest way to find the Mode is to /**View** the data in a bar chart. The modal value is the highest bar.

The **Median** is the middle value in the set, when the values have been arranged into size order. So, the median value in the set 1, 1, 3, 5, 7, 8, 8, 9, 14 is '7'. SuperCalc3 can help you to find the median of a range, using the command /**Arrange**. This will take a given range of values in a Row or Column (or a part of one) and sort them into either ascending or descending order.

In this particular case, the command would be:

/Arrange,Column,**B,3:14,A**scending,**Y**es

The /**Arrange** command does not just move the individual cells in a column, but whole rows right across the spreadsheet. Similarly, arranging on the basis of one row will rearrange the order of the columns. Any formula outside of the rearranged area can be confused by this; here, for example, the SUM ranges would need to be rewritten as the cells that they referenced would no longer be at the ends of the range. So use the command sparingly.

Arrange is more commonly used with the data management facilities, and is covered more fully in Section 44.

■ SECTION 40
Moving averages

Here we have a good example of how simple statistical techniques can help to show the underlying trends in a business.

```
   :  A  ::  B  ::  C  :     :  A  ::  B  ::  C  ::  D  :
 1|DRINKS SALES            21|Jul         338
 2|                        22|Aug         309
 3|Jan 84     234          23|Sep         235
 4|Feb        196          24|Oct         222
 5|Mar        216          25|Nov         218
 6|Apr        217          26|Dec         303
 7|May        244          27|Jan 86      247
 8|Jun        316          28|Feb         262
 9|Jul        339          29|Mar         260
10|Aug        246          30|Apr         233
11|Sep        240          31|May         238
12|Oct        221          32|Jun         313
13|Nov        216          33|Jul         299
14|Dec        282          34|Aug         222
15|Jan 85     247          35|Sep         235
16|Feb        254          36|Oct         210
17|Mar        257          37|Nov         214
18|Apr        226          38|Dec         271
19|May        271          39|
20|Jun        312          40|
 v C40
Width:  9  Memory: 62 Last Col/Row:B38   ? for HELP
   1>
F1 = Help; F2 = Erase Line/Return to Spreadsheet; F9 = Plot; F10 = View
```

The figure above shows the monthly sales figures over three years for a soft drinks firm. If the figures are turned into a line graph, their seasonal pattern becomes very clear but the overall trend of the business is far less visible as shown overleaf.

DRINKS SALES

What is needed is some means of smoothing out the seasonal variations. This can be done in either of two ways:

A **Cumulative 12-month Total** will show the sales for the previous year, looking back from each month – JAN – DEC, FEB – JAN, etc. On the spreadsheet above, these start in C17 with **SUM(B5:B16)** and carry on down from there with adjusted ranges, so that C18 contains **SUM(B6:B17)**.

A **Moving average** finds the average of the previous 12 months' figures in a similar fashion. The formula in D17, for instance, is **AV(B5:B16)**. The advantage of using an Average, as against a Total, is that the results are in the same scale as the original monthly figures, and can be plotted against them meaningfully as shown on page 164.

■ SECTION 40
Moving averages

	A		B			C			D	
1	MOVING AVERAGES									
2						Cumulative			Moving	
3						Total			Averages	
4	Jan 84		234							
5	Feb		196							
6	Mar		216							
7	Apr		217							
8	May		244							
9	Jun		316							
10	Jul		339							
11	Aug		246							
12	Sep		240							
13	Oct		221							
14	Nov		216							
15	Dec		282							
16	Jan 85		247			2967			247.25	
17	Feb		254			2980			248.33	
18	Mar		257			3038			253.17	
19	Apr		226			3079			256.58	
20	May		271			3088			257.33	
21	Jun		312			3115			259.58	
22	Jul		338			3111			259.25	
23	Aug		309			3110			259.17	
24	Sep		235			3173			264.42	
25	Oct		222			3168			264.00	
26	Nov		218			3169			264.08	
27	Dec		303			3171			264.25	
28	Jan 86		247			3192			266.00	
29	Feb		262			3192			266.00	
30	Mar		260			3200			266.67	
31	Apr		233			3203			266.92	
32	May		238			3210			267.50	
33	Jun		313			3177			264.75	
34	Jul		299			3178			264.83	
35	Aug		222			3139			261.58	
36	Sep		235			3052			254.33	
37	Oct		210			3052			254.33	
38	Nov		214			3040			253.33	
39	Dec		271			3036			253.00	
40										

Moving averages

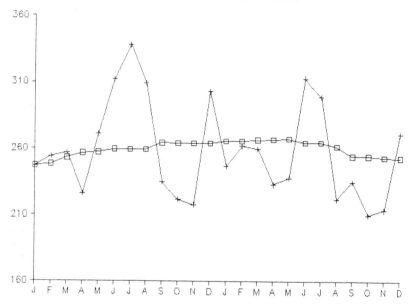

MOVING AVERAGES

Normal distribution and standard deviation

The various average figures can give us some idea about a set of data, but only a restricted one. The two sets 5,6,7,8,9 and 1,3,7,11,13 both have the same mean of 7, but have completely different spreads. In the first set, none of the values are more than 2 away from the mean, while in the second set the extremes are 6 different.

Whenever we collect data concerned with variation in a population — whether heights or dress sizes of women, or the weight of jam in the jars on a factory production line — the graph that can be drawn from it will generally show a **Normal Distribution**. Most readings cluster around an average, and as you get further from the average, so you find fewer items. The average height for women is around 5 foot 4 inches; most are between 5 foot and 5 foot 8 inches; very few indeed are more than a foot different from the average.

Statisticians use the **Standard Deviation** to describe the spread of values. It is a calculation based on the difference between the mean and the actual values of the items in the set. The relationship between the Normal distribution and standard deviation is shown here:

The Normal distribution

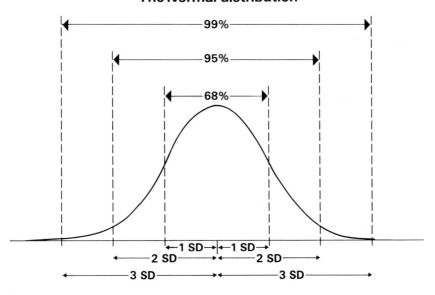

■ SECTION 41
Normal distribution and standard deviation

In a Normal distribution you would expect to find:

68% within 1 SD more or less than the Mean
95% within 2 SD more or less than the Mean
99.9% within 3 SD more or less than the Mean

To calculate the standard deviation you need to go through these stages.

■ Find the Mean value.

■ Find the deviation of each value from the mean (value − mean).

■ Square each of these deviation results.

■ Find the mean of the squares.

■ Find the square root of the mean of the squares.

The illustration below shows how SuperCalc3 can be used to calculate standard deviations. (Ignore for the moment the formulae listed under **Central Range**. We will return to them later.)

The **Numbers** to be processed are entered into Column A. Here we are using only 20 readings, but the spreadsheet can accommodate up to 250 down its rows. At the bottom of that column, the AV function is used to find the Mean.

Column B calculates the Deviations from the Mean by taking each of the column A numbers from the Mean. The resulting value is then squared in column C. At the foot of this column you will see that **AV** is used to get the mean of these squares. The function **SQRT** finds the SQare RooT of the mean in cell C26. This is the Standard Deviation.

The numbers that were keyed in to test the formula produced a mean value of 11.7 and a standard deviation of 1.73. If those numbers have a Normal distribution, then 68% should fall between 11.7 − 1.73 (9.97) and 11.7 + 1.73 (13.43). This is tested on the sheet by the formulae shown under the heading **Central Range**. They are a variation on those used earlier to group readings.

IF(AND(A3> = C28,A3< = E28),TRUE,FALSE)

This compares the number in column A with the limits held in cells C28 and E28. If it falls within the limits, the value **TRUE** is allocated to the D3; if not **FALSE** will be returned. **TRUE** and **FALSE** are **logical values**. They are displayed on the sheet as '1' or '0' and may be added to find the total of TRUE results.

Normal distribution and standard deviation

	A	B	C	D	E	F	G
1	STANDARD DEVIATION						
2	Numbers	Deviation	Dev^2	Central Range			
3	14	A3-A25	B3^2	IF(AND(A3>=C28,A3<=E28),TRUE,FALSE)			
4	12	A4-A25	B4^2	IF(AND(A4>=C28,A4<=E28),TRUE,FALSE)			
5	9	A5-A25	B5^2	IF(AND(A5>=C28,A5<=E28),TRUE,FALSE)			
6	12	A6-A25	B6^2	IF(AND(A6>=C28,A6<=E28),TRUE,FALSE)			
7	11	A7-A25	B7^2	IF(AND(A7>=C28,A7<=E28),TRUE,FALSE)			
8	13	A8-A25	B8^2	IF(AND(A8>=C28,A8<=E28),TRUE,FALSE)			
9	14	A9-A25	B9^2	IF(AND(A9>=C28,A9<=E28),TRUE,FALSE)			
10	11	A10-A25	B10^2	IF(AND(A10>=C28,A10<=E28),TRUE,FALSE)			
11	12	A11-A25	B11^2	IF(AND(A11>=C28,A11<=E28),TRUE,FALSE)			
12	11	A12-A25	B12^2	IF(AND(A12>=C28,A12<=E28),TRUE,FALSE)			
13	12	A13-A25	B13^2	IF(AND(A13>=C28,A13<=E28),TRUE,FALSE)			
14	13	A14-A25	B14^2	IF(AND(A14>=C28,A14<=E28),TRUE,FALSE)			
15	12	A15-A25	B15^2	IF(AND(A15>=C28,A15<=E28),TRUE,FALSE)			
16	13	A16-A25	B16^2	IF(AND(A16>=C28,A16<=E28),TRUE,FALSE)			
17	11	A17-A25	B17^2	IF(AND(A17>=C28,A17<=E28),TRUE,FALSE)			
18	15	A18-A25	B18^2	IF(AND(A18>=C28,A18<=E28),TRUE,FALSE)			
19	10	A19-A25	B19^2	IF(AND(A19>=C28,A19<=E28),TRUE,FALSE)			
20	9	A20-A25	B20^2	IF(AND(A20>=C28,A20<=E28),TRUE,FALSE)			
21	8	A21-A25	B21^2	IF(AND(A21>=C28,A21<=E28),TRUE,FALSE)			
22	12	A22-A25	B22^2	IF(AND(A22>=C28,A22<=E28),TRUE,FALSE)			
23							
24	Mean of values		Mean of squares				
25	AV(A3:A22)		AV(C3:C22)				
26	Standard Deviation = SQRT(C25)						
27							
28	68% expected between A25-C26			and	A25+C26		
29	Actual percentage		SUM(D3:D22)/20*100				
30							
31	Standard Error		C26/SQRT(20)				
32	95% prob. true mean A25-2*C31			and	A31+2*C31		

■ SECTION 42
Sampling and quality control

There are two rows at the bottom of the spreadsheet in the previous section that were not covered there. They are both concerned with the reliability of samples.

Quality control is an important part of any manufacturing process. You must check that goods are fit for sale; that packets and jars contain the weights that they are supposed to; that equipment will last for the required length of time. It is frequently not feasible to check or test every individual item – impossible if it involves testing to destruction! – so sampling is the normal practice.

This is where the statistical methods come into play. How many items do you need to test to get a sufficiently reliable measure of quality? The **Standard Error** is a key concept in this. It gives a guide to the accuracy of the Mean produced by the sample. It is calculated by dividing the standard deviation by the square root of the number of items in the sample. In the example mentioned, the formulae is:

C26/SQRT(20)

It produces the value .39.

The standard error is smaller with larger samples. Thus, with a standard deviation of 2 and a sample of 16, the standard error would be 2/SQRT(16) = 2/4 or 0.5. If the sample were 36, rather than 16, but with the same standard deviation, the standard error would be 3/SQRT(36) = 2/6 or 0.33.

The possibility of error can be reduced more rapidly by taking two separate samples, finding the standard error of each, and then multiplying these together. Thus if two samples both give a standard error of 0.5, the overall error is $0.5 \times 0.5 = 0.25$. Compare this with the 0.33 produced by the larger, single sample, and you will see that statistically you will get more reliable results from several small samples than from one large one.

The relationship between the standard error and the true mean is like that of the Normal distribution and standard deviation.

There is a 68% probability that the true mean will be within 1 standard error of the sample mean; a 95% probability that it will be within 2 standard errors, and a 99.9% probability that it will be within 3 standard errors.

PART EIGHT

Data management

The database concept

SuperCalc3's data management functions allow you to use the spreadsheet as a database, i.e. for the storage and retrieval of information of any kind. It could be used in place of a card index system or address book, as will be seen in Section 46; but the data management facilities may also be combined with the normal spreadsheet calculations to provide a very powerful utility. The 'SuperCalc3 Phone Book' and the credit control sheet developed later should give you some idea of what can be achieved by combining these two aspects of the software.

In a database, information is organised into **records** and **fields**. A record can be thought of as a card in a card index system. It holds all the information about one individual, company, product or whatever. The record is subdivided into fields, in the same way that a card will be marked out into areas or lines in which particular items must be written. On the spreadsheet, each record occupies a whole row, and the cells are the fields. The cells in any given column would normally hold the same type of data for each record, and the names given to fields are important as they are used in some of the search routines.

```
           !   A   !!   B   !!   C   !!   D   !
        _ 1|NAME     TEL NUM  ADDRESS 1ADDRESS 2
        / 2|A.E Smith01-234-5643 ThornhSouth Par
Records-- 3|Wilbur Wh0105-987-The KnollLittle Sa
        \_ 4|Jones Bro221116   17a High Warminste
```

(The rather cluttered appearance of the above is to remind you that the text that is written into a cell may be far longer than the display width. It can always be transferred to wider cells, or be allowed to spread across blank ones if you need to display it in full.)

Databases have become one of the most widely used business computing tools, for computerised data handling can be so much more efficient than paper-based files. They take far less time to maintain and to use. New entries can be quickly slotted into the right place, for the computer does any sorting that is required, and a single file can be re-organised to produce lists in different orders – alphabetical, by type, by town or whatever. Updating old records is simply a matter of getting the computer to find the one, or the set, that you want, and writing in any alterations – and, unlike cards, you do not finish up with a mess of Tipp-Ex or crossings-out on regularly updated entries. If the database is also able to handle calculations – which is very much the case with SuperCalc3 – then it can be used as part of an accounting or stock control system.

■ SECTION 43
The database concept

The 'Database' database − a worked example

Over the rest of this section, and in the next, we will explore the data management commands by creating and using a simple database. It will store information about some of the commercial databases that are currently on the market.

```
 !   A    !!   B   !!    C     !!    D      !!   E    !
 1!DATABASE
 2!INPUT RANGE  B4 to E10
 3!-------------------------------------------------------------------
 4!Title Line  Name       Price        Publisher     Tel Num        !
 5!------------ AT LAST                29.95Advance Software0279 412441 !
 6!             CAMBASE                49.95Camsoft        0766 831878 !
 7!             CARDBOX PLUS           60.00Caxton Software 01-379 6502 !
 8!Records      DATAFLOW II            49.95Micro Power    0532 458800 !
 9!             DBASE II              120.00Ashton Tate    0628 33123  !
10!             CONDOR                 90.00Caxton Software 01-379 6502 !
11!-------------------------------------------------------------------
```

SuperCalc3's data management commands are all accessed via the slash command //**Data** − note the double slash. The next level of commands are then displayed in the prompt line:

I(nput),C(riterion),O(utput),F(ind),E(xtract),S(elect,R(emain)?

You must start with **Input**. This is used to define the **INPUT RANGE** − the block of cells in which the records are to be stored. It may be redefined later, if you need to add more records or fields, but it must be there before you can perform any other Data commands.

SuperCalc3 assumes that field names will be written on the top row of the input area. If you are going to use the database in such a way that field names are not needed − an unlikely event − then the top row may be left blank, but it may not be used for data. Anything written there will be treated as a field name.

We only want to hold the records on half a dozen databases, so seven rows will be sufficient for our input range. For each one we will store **Name, Price, Publisher** and **Tel Num**, so four columns are required. The range can be set up with the command:

//Data,Input,**B4:E10**

The database concept

After you have pressed RETURN you will see that the Entry line still displays //**Data**. Most of the sub-commands will return to this level.

Once the input range has been defined, you can start keying in the data for the records. With a large database it is a good idea to write in only a selection of the records at first. These can then be used to test the database in action. If it will not do what you want it to do, then it may be necessary to redesign it − and the data may then need to be retyped. Type in the details of the six software packages shown in the illustration above. Time now to start using the commands that will sort and search the database.

■ SECTION 44
Sorting and searching

The command that is used for sorting a set of records into order is the same one that is used for any rearranging in SuperCalc3 – /**Arrange**. This will take the items in a row or column and sort them into alphabetical, numeric or date order.

When it sorts down a column though, it does not just re-order the cells in that column, it re-orders the whole rows right across the spreadsheet. This is, of course, what you want it to do within the database structure, for it means that whole records are sorted on the basis of any field. In an ordinary spreadsheet, Arrange must be used with care, as it is all too easy to set out to re-order a single column of figures, only to discover that you have thoroughly disorganised off-screen areas of the sheet.

Test out Arrange on the records that have been typed into the Input Area. The following sequence will bring them into 'Price' order.

/Arrange,Column,C__

You will now be asked for **Row range?**. The records to be sorted are between 5 and 10; type in **5:10** and you will be faced with the next option:

A(scending) or D(escending)?

If Ascending order is selected, the highest value will be at the bottom of the list on screen. The last stage in this routine asks you whether or not formula should be adjusted as the rows are re-organised. If your records include formulae, then select **Yes** as otherwise the cell references will no longer apply. Where there are no formulae the quicker **No Adjust** option is to be preferred.

Your finished Entry line should look like this:

/Arrange,Column,**C,5:10,**Ascending,**No**

Searching

The **CRITERION RANGE** defines an area where you will give the details of the items that you are looking for. These will be the criteria that SuperCalc3 will base its searches on. The size of the Criterion Range depends upon the type of search that you want to perform.

Sorting and searching

```
  !    A    !!    B    !!    C    !!    D    !!    E    !
 1!DATABASE
 2!INPUT RANGE  B4 to E10
 3!---------------------------------------------------------------
 4!Title Line   Name        Price        Publisher       Tel Num    !
 5!------------ AT LAST      29.95        Advance Software0279 412441 !
 6!             CAMBASE      49.95        Camsoft         0766 831878 !
 7!             CARDBOX PLUS 60.00        Caxton Software 01-379 6502 !
 8!Records      DATAFLOW II  49.95        Micro Power     0532 458800 !
 9!             DBASE II     120.00       Ashton Tate     0628 33123  !
10!             CONDOR       90.00        Caxton Software 01-379 6502 !
11!---------------------------------------------------------------
12!CRITERION RANGE  B14 to C15 or C16
13!-------------------------------------------
14!Title Line   Name        Price        !
15!Search Data  CA*          C5<90        !
16!  "     "                              :
17!-------------------------------------------
```

The simplest type of search uses only a single criterion, e.g. to find all the databases that cost less than £50. To do this we will set up a Criterion Range of one column and **TWO** rows. The extra (top) row is essential. It is where the field name will be written.

//Data,Criterion,**B14:B15**

Press RETURN twice to get out of the //**Data** Entry line, then type 'Price' in B14, writing it as it appears in the input range; and the formula **C5<50** in B15. This is the test that will be performed in the entries in column C of the database. The formula is always written with reference to the first record in the input range.

To perform the search, use the command sequence:

//**D**ata,Find

Any records where the 'Price' value is less than £50 will be highlighted in turn. Use the up and down arrow keys to move backwards and forwards through the matching records. The left/right arrow keys are also active at this stage, and can be used to move the cursor from one field to the next within a record. This allows you to read through those records that are too long to fit on the screen, and to position the cursor for updating an entry.

Sorting and searching

Press RETURN to exit from the search, and you will find that the spreadsheet cursor is wherever you left the search cursor. If at that point, you select the **R(emain)** sub-command, the spreadsheet cursor will stay on that cell. Press RETURN instead, and the cursor will jump back to wherever it was before the **Find** was performed.

Text-based searches are slightly different. There it is not necessary to write a formula. Just write the item that you are looking for under the field name.

```
    :  A  ::  B  :
14|        Publisher
15|        CAMSOFT
```

The search criteria must be written in the same way as the entry. SuperCalc3 will not find 'CAMSOFT' if it has been told to look for 'Camsoft'.

Where you want to find a set of entries, **wildcards** may be used. These are symbols that, like the wildcards or jokers in a pack of playing cards, may stand for any other character.

? will replace any individual character, and * accepts any ending to a string. So, if you specify 'C*' under the field 'Name', the search will find any entry that starts with 'C', no matter how long it is — 'CAMBASE', 'CARDBOX' and 'CONDOR'. Similarly, the criteria '???ton*' under the heading 'Publisher' will find any entry that has three letters before 'ton' — 'Ash**ton** Tate' and 'Cax**ton** Software'.

There is a third symbol that may be used in text searches. A tilde ~ before the text will find records that do *not* match the details given. So ~ **C*** will find those that do not start with 'C'.

The field name may be left blank. If it is, then the search will be performed on every field in each record.

Multiple criteria

You can extend the Criterion Range to two columns and specify two criteria for your search. Here the range is B14:C15:

```
    :  A  ::   B   ::  C  :
14|        Publisher   Price
15|        A*          C5<100
```

Sorting and searching

Both of the conditions must be satisfied in this type of search. In this case, when a /**Find** is performed it will pick out AT LAST, the only database under £100, and where the publisher starts with A.

The Criterion Range can be extended downwards where different alternatives are being sought in each field. The Criterion Range must be set to B14:C16 before this search is started.

```
       !  A   !!     B        !!   C.  !
  14|          Publisher      Price
  15|          A*             C5<100
  16|          D*             C5<100
```

This will find AT LAST and DATAFLOW II.

■ SECTION 45
Reporting out

The /**Find** command is a useful means of tracking down records for updating, or for immediate reference, but it if you want printed output (reports) from the database you should use other data management commands.

```
    :   A    ::   B    ::     C     ::      D      ::    E    :
18:OUTPUT RANGE   B19 to E24
19:------------------------------------------------------------------
20:          CAMBASE              49.95Camsoft         0766 831878  :
21:          CARDBOX PLUS         60.00Caxton Software 01-379 6502  :
22:                                                                 :
23:                                                                 :
24:                                                                 :
```

First you must define an **OUTPUT RANGE**. This is where records will be written as they are found by the searches. It must contain the same number of columns as the input range, and, as with the other ranges, the top row is for field names. If it is left blank, then records will be written there in the same field order that they appear in the input range. If you want a selective Output, then write the names of the fields that you want to see (in any order) into that top row. The Output Range should have sufficient rows to accommodate the largest number of records that are likely to be written at any one time. Here it is defined as six rows and four columns by this command sequence:

//Data,Output,**B19:E24**

Either **Extract** and **Select** can be used to search the database and transfer records to the Output Range. Both need the Criterion Range to be set up as it is for a Find command. The only difference between them is that **Extract** will automatically transfer each matching record, but **Select** will first display each, on a highlight bar, and ask if it is wanted.

Once a set of records have been copied into the Output Range, they can be re-ordered if necessary, using /**Arrange**, before being printed out with the normal /**Output** command.

The SuperCalc3 phone book

The task

The sheet should store names, phone numbers and area (charge) codes in a database. As well as acting as a phone book, it should also be able to calculate the cost of a call on the basis of the length of the call, and the time of the day.

The design

The illustration below shows the basic layout of the sheet. It may be considered in five areas. The first three, in the block from A1 to F17, will be visible on screen during normal use. The others will only be brought into view when they need updating.

The **Input Range** is here labelled **Who to Find**. A single entry is needed in the cell below the field heading **NAME**.

The **Output Range** in A7:C8 has been defined at one row deep, as only one number will be wanted at any time. The //**Data, Select** command will be used for all searches.

Immediately below this is the area in which the cost of the phone calls is calculated. The user is expected to enter the time and charge code — the codes are shown to the side for ready reference. We will return shortly to the formulae that are used in this part of the sheet.

The **Input Range** has been defined at the bottom of the sheet. It is three columns wide, and as deep as need be. In the 'Database' database that was explored in the last few sections, the input range was at the top of the sheet. This was because it was the part that had to be tackled first. In practice, it is better to site it at the bottom. It can be extended more easily there, and it leaves the top section for the criterion and output ranges, which are accessed more often.

The final part of this sheet is a reference table headed **TIME PER UNIT**. This is composed of three lookup tables, each of which shows the number of seconds that make up a charge unit in the three different time bands.

The phone book in use

The user, or perhaps we should say the operator, starts by entering the name of the person to find in cell B5. The search is then performed by the command:

//**D**ata,Select

	A	B	C	D	E	F	G	H	I	J	K
1	TELEPHONE PAD								TIME PER UNIT		
2											
3	Who to Find										
4	NAME				AREA CODING	Cheap		Standard		Peak	
5	Jim*				Local	1	360	1	90	1	60
6	-----				Rate A	2	100	2	34.3	2	25.7
7	Name	Number	Rate		Rate B1	3	60	3	30	3	22.5
8					Rate b	4	45	4	24	4	18
9	Jim Jones	0703 98765	1		Ireland	5	12	5	8	5	8
10					Mobile	6	12	6	8	6	8
11	TIME in Mins...		15								
12	CHARGE CODE(1,2,3)		3								
13	-----				CHARGE RATE CODING						
14	Secs. per unit		60		Weekend/evening	1		UNIT COST			
15	UNITS		15		Wkday 8-9am/1-6pm	2			4.4		
16	COST		.66		Weekday 9am-1pm	3					
17	-----										
18	DIRECTORY										
19	NAME	NUMBER	RATE		AREA CODING						
20	Jim Jones	0703 98765	1		Local	1					
21	Mum	0472 123456	4		Rate A	2					
22	Uncle Harry	01 999-3366	3		Rate B1	3					
23	Newtech	0276 685996	2		Rate b	4					
24	R.D.Hogg	0860 54321	6		Ireland	5					
25	Seamus McGuiness	010 353 903 123	5		Mobile	6					

The SuperCalc3 phone book

When the right record is highlighted, it is copied to the Output Range, and the search is ended. Notice that cell C9 will now hold the Area Code for calculating the cost of the call.

At the end of the call, its duration and charge code are entered into cells B11 and B12. The spreadsheet then performs the following command to get the **TIME PER UNIT** from the appropriate lookup table.

IF(B12 = 1,LOOKUP(C9,F4:F9),IF(B12 = 2,LOOKUP(C9,H4:H9), LOOKUP(C9,J4:J9)))

It is an ungainly formula, but it works! Take the example of a Rate B call during a weekday afternoon. The Charge Code in B12 will be 2, so the second lookup will be performed on the table at H4:H9. The Area Code in C9 is 4, so the value found for Time Per Unit will be 24.

The **UNITS** in B15 are calculated by this formula:

ROUND(B11*60/B14,0)

This converts the **TIME in Mins** into seconds − **B11*60** − then divides it by the seconds per unit figure from B14. The **ROUND** function reduces any value to a given number of decimal places. So, ROUND(123.4567,2) specifies two decimal places, and would give '123.46' − notice that the last digit has been rounded up as it was followed by a value of 5 or more. Here we must work in whole units, so the formula requests '0' decimal places.

The last part of the cost calculation is to multiply the number of units by the current cost per unit. This figure is held in cell I14, beneath the lookup tables. The formula divides the result by 100, so that the value is shown in pounds and pence:

B15*I14/100

Try it. Use it regularly to monitor the cost of your calls, and it could encourage sufficiently economical use of the telephone to pay for the cost of your computer − in the end!

■ SECTION 47
Credit control

In this last example of data management, we will look at combining the facilities with a more traditional spreadsheet application.

The Task

To maintain a summarised record of customers' accounts so that tighter control may be exercised over the credit extended by the company. The sheet should be used for calculating the figures for the accounts and provide a simple means of extracting up-to-date information on any individual or set of customers. It will also be required to keep totals of the accounts.

The Design

The figure below shows the layout of a simplified sheet. It holds for each customer the accounts for the current and previous month ('Old..' and 'New..'). The figures record the opening balance, debt incurred and amount paid for each month, and the current balance of the account. Each column of the accounts is totalled by a SUM formula in row 21.

```
    :     A    ::  B  ::  C  ::  D  ::  E  ::  F  ::  G  ::  H  ::   I
 1:CUSTOMER ACCOUNTS
 2:CRITERION AREA
 3:Old Bal.       Current Balance
 4:               1       1
 5:
 6:OUTPUT AREA
 7:Name           Old Bal.New Bal Current Balance
 8:Mercurian PP    -2500   -4000   -4000
 9:National Widget  -500       0    -750
10:R & J Brown      -200    -250    -150
11:
12:INPUT AREA
13:Name           Old Bal.Old Dbt Old Cr. New Bal New Dbt New Cr. Current Balance
14:
15:Mercurian PP    -2500    4500    3000   -4000       0       0   -4000
16:National Widget  -500    2000    2500       0     750       0    -750
17:Hilltop Press       0     375       0    -375     500     425    -450
18:R & J Brown      -200     450     400    -250     250     350    -150
19:Smith Bros          0     150     125     -25     125       0    -150
20:
21:TOTALS          -3200    7475    6025   -4650    1625     775   -5500
```

You should notice that the input range has an additional blank row at the top and at the bottom. It is the cells in these rows that are referenced in the SUM formulae in the TOTALS line. The active rows — 15 to 19 — may now be reorganised by an Arrange command without corrupting the formulae.

In the sheet as shown, the /**Arrange** command has been used to put the customers in Ascending order of **Current balance**, so that the worst payer appears at the top of the list. It may be noted that the firm appears to have suspended its trading with Mercurian Pulp Products for the time being.

The field names **Old Bal.** and **Current balance** have been entered into the Criterion Range, along with the formulae **B14<0** and **H14<0**. (These will actually be displayed as either '1' or '0' depending upon whether or not the tests are true in the specified cells.)

When //**Data,Extract** is performed, the search will output any firm that owed money at the start of the previous month, and that currently owes money.

The Output Range has been headed up so that only those aspects of the account that are under scrutiny — the balances — will be copied into the range.

By altering the Criterion Range details, and the headings of the Output Range, different aspects of the accounts can be brought out for examination. If there are a significant number of customers, the process will be far quicker — and more reliable — than reading through the files to check the figures.

PART NINE

Spreadsheet mathematics

Algebra and equations

If you have a problem that can be expressed mathematically as an algebraic equation, there is usually a way of solving it on the spreadsheet. It may be a matter of converting the equation into a spreadsheet formula, of producing an appropriate graph or of developing an algorithm — a series of formulae. Over the next three sections we will explore these alternative approaches to spreadsheet mathematics.

Quadratic equations

What this example shows is that is is easy to solve an algebraic problem on the spreadsheet as long as you can find an equation to describe the unknown quantity.

All quadratic equations take the form:

$$ax^2 + bx + c = 0$$

where a, b and c are all number values, and the highest power of x is a square. The problem is to find the values for x — there are always two — which will solve the equation.

```
      |    A   :: B   :: C   :: D   :: E  :
 1 :EQUATIONS
 2 :
 3 :Quadratic Equations
 4 :Where equation has the form ax^2 + bx + c = 0
 5 :Use the formula:     x = -b + or - sqrt(b^2 - 4a
 6 :                          --------------------------
 7 :                                 2a
 8 :e.g. 3x^2 + 9x - 12 = 0
 9 : a = 3 : b = 9 : c = -12
10 :
11 :Data Entry
12 :a          b        c
13 : 3         9       -12
14 :
15 :Formula
16 :(i) x = (-B12+SQRT(B12^2-4*A12*C12))/(2*A12)
17 :(ii) x = (-B12-SQRT(B12^2-4*A12*C12))/(2*A12)
18 :gives x (i)              1
19 :      x (ii)            -4
20 :
```

Algebra and equations

In this form, the spreadsheet cannot tackle it by a numeric method, but the equation can be transposed into the form:

$$x = \frac{-b \pm \sqrt{(b^2 - 4ac)}}{2a}$$

This equation can be easily converted to two spreadsheet formulae (one for each of the + or − versions) to find the values of x. You can see this at work in this illustration.

The formula have been written for general use, in that the number values are all entered via cells. If the purpose of the spreadsheet was to solve a specific equation, it would have been simpler to write them directly into the formula. Thus, the equation:

$3x^2 + 9x - 12 = 0$

could have been solved by the formulae:

(−9 + SQRT(9 ^ 2 − 4*3* − 12))/(2*3)
(−9 − SQRT(9 ^ 2 − 4*3* − 12))/(2*3)

■ SECTION 48
Algebra and equations

Graphed solutions

To produce a graph you first need a range of values. If these have to be worked out by hand, or individually on a calculator, then it can make graphing very slow. With the spreadsheet of course, the whole process is made much simpler.

```
      :   A   ::  B   ::  C   ::  D   ::  E   :
   1 :BY GRAPHING
   2 :Equation    y = 3x^2+9x-12
   3 :initial x        -8
   4 :x increment       1
   5 :         x        y
   6 :        -8       108   =   3*A6^2+9*A6-12
   7 :        -7        72
   8 :        -6        42
   9 :        -5        18
  10 :        -4         0
  11 :        -3       -12
  12 :        -2       -18
  13 :        -1       -18
  14 :         0       -12
  15 :         1         0
  16 :         2        18
  17 :         3        42
  18 :         4        72
  19 :         5       108
  20 :         6       150
```

The first step is to set up a range of x values. As you may not know what range of values are actually needed, then you need to write flexibility into the sheet from the start. In the figure above you will see that the **initial x** value is entered into the cell B3, and the increment for the series into B4. The range of values is then produced in cells A6:A20 by formulae that add the increment onto the previous value. The equation $y = 3x^2 + 9x - 12$ is translated into a formula in cell B6. Its value will depend upon the x value in cell A6.

```
    :  A   ::     B       :
  6 : B3       3*A6^2+9*A6-12
  7 : A6+B4    3*A7^2+9*A7-12
  8 : A7+B4    3*A8^2+9*A8-12
```

186

■ SECTION 48
Algebra and equations

Replication will soon build the whole table.

To turn these figures into a graph, the only essential requirement is that you give the data range with the command:

   /View,Data,**B6:B20**

Press F10, and you will get a graph like that below. The two possible values of *x* can be read off where the line crosses the horizontal axis. If the line does not cross the axis on the graph, then return to the sheet and alter the initial *x* value and increment to bring it on screen. For more accurate results, you can select an *x* value that you can see is close to the crossing point and give a very small increment.

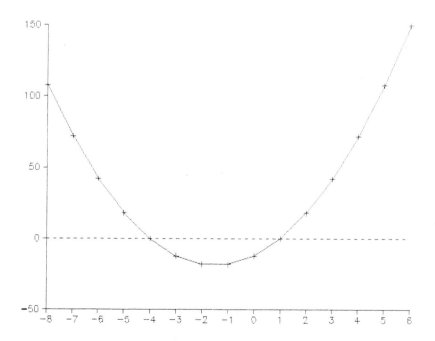

High-resolution graphics

SuperCalc3's graphic outputs are designed to make best use of the media available, and this applies as much to monitors as it does to printers and plotters. If the system has a colour monitor, then colour will normally be used to give greater impact to displays. With a black and white monitor, the high resolution of the screen is put to full use to create more detailed, and more accurate graphs.

If you have a colour monitor, and want to produce graphs where accuracy is more important than impact, then you can ask SuperCalc3 to treat the monitor as if it were monochrome. To do this, call up the Graphics and Device Options screen with the command:

/Global,Graphics,Options

```
GRAPHICS AND DEVICE OPTIONS

Appearance Features:              For graphics printers:
Grids          N                  Resolution        S
Axes           Y
Ticks          Y                  For pen plotters:
Graph Box      N                  Num. pens         1

For Pie, Bar and Stacked-Bar:     Plotter Interface:
Fill Type      S                  Use               P

For Line, Hi-Lo, Area and X-Y:    Parallel Options:
Point Markers  Y                  Printer number    1
Lines          Y
                                  Serial Options:
GRAPHIC DEVICE SETTINGS:          Com number        1
                                  Baud Rate      4800
Console:                          Parity            N
Monitor        C                  Data bits         8
                                  Stop bits         1


H(orizontal), V(ertical), N(either) or B(oth)?
 25>/Global,Graphics,Options
 F1 = Help; F2 = Erase Line/Return to Spreadsheet; F9 = Plot; F10 = View
```

■ SECTION 49
Graphs make sense

Move the highlight bar down to the **Monitor** line and select **B** to switch to the Black/White setting. While you are on this screen you might also like to note, and to select, those options that control the appearance of graphs. **Grids** can make it easier to read values off a graph. The suitability of other options depends very much on the nature of the graphs.

Economic order quantity (EOQ)

This second example is an interesting one for it shows that a numeric solution, though accurate, may actually be less satisfactory than a graphical one.

The problem is to find the most economic quantity of a stock to order at any one time. It is assumed for this that the cost of ordering, the cost of carrying the stock and its annual demand are all known. The formula that gives the economic order cost is:

SQRT(2*Cost of ordering*Demand/Cost of carrying)

	A	B	C	D	E	F	G	H	I
1	ECONOMIC ORDER QUANTITY								
2	Annual Usage	10000							
3	Unit Price	10							
4	Carrying cost	1							
5	Ordering cost	75							
6									
7	BY FORMULA	= SQRT(2*B5*B2/B4)							
8	EOQ =	1224.7							
9									
10									
11									
12	ORDER QUANTITY	400	800	1600	2400	3200	4000	4800	5600
13	NO. OF ORDERS	25	12.5	6.25	4.1667	3.125	2.5	2.0833	1.7857
14	ORDERING COST	1875	937.5	468.75	312.5	234.38	187.5	156.25	133.93
15	AVERAGE STOCK	200	400	800	1200	1600	2000	2400	2800
16	CARRYING COST	200	400	800	1200	1600	2000	2400	2800
17	TOTAL COST	2075	1337.5	1268.8	1512.5	1834.4	2187.5	2556.3	2933.9
18									

This has been converted to a SuperCalc3 formula in row 8 of the above spreadsheet, and gives a value of 1224.7. What it does not tell you is how much leeway you have. Will it be very much more expensive to order

Graphs make sense

in quantities of 1000 or less? There may well be cash-flow considerations that would make a smaller quantity more attractive. Equally, there may be bulk discounts to be gained by going up to 1500? How far would that be an uneconomic quantity?

These questions can be answered more satisfactorily by tackling the problem graphically. To do it we need to generate ranges of values for the costs that are involved. This is done in the table at the bottom of the spreadsheet.

Ordering cost is found by multiplying the average number of orders per year by the cost of each order. The number of orders is itself the result of dividing the annual demand by the order size.

Carrying cost is the product of average stock (order quantity/2) and the unit carrying cost.

Total cost is the sum of the other two.

The figures in rows 14, 16 and 17 are selected as data for the graph. The result is shown below. In this example, it is apparent that the total costs are pretty much the same over the range 1000 to 1500. Other factors, such as storage space and bulk purchase discounts can now be considered before a final decision is made.

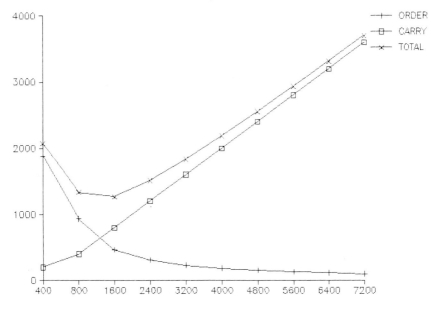

■ SECTION 50
Spreadsheet algorithms

In the last of these three examples we will use a series of formula to achieve a solution of a problem where there are two unknown quantities – the simultaneous equation.

In mathematics there are several ways of tackling simultaneous equations. The spreadsheet shown below is based on the algorithm used in the elimination method. This works by removing one of the unknown factors from the equations, so that the second can be found. Its value can then be written back into the original equations to find the other unknown.

Step 1

The two equations are each multiplied throughout by the x value of the opposite equation:

(i) $3x + 2y = 17$
(ii) $5x - 3y = 22$

(i) $15x + 10y = 85$ (multiplied by 5)

(ii) $15x - 9y = 66$ (multiplied by 3)

Step 2

The values in the second equation are then taken from those in the first, so that x is eliminated from the problem:

$19y = 19$ (after subtracting (ii) from (i))

Step 3

The value of y can then be found by dividing its number into the figure on the right-hand side:

$y = 19/19$
$\quad = 1$

Step 4

The y value can then be substituted back into the first equation to find the value for x:

$3x + 2y = 17$, so
$x = (17 - 2*1)/3$
$\quad = 5$

Spreadsheet algorithms

This process can be translated directly into a series of simple SuperCalc3 formulae, as you can see below:

```
 !  A  !!  B  !!  C  !!  D  !        !  A  !!  B  !!  C  !
 1|SIMULTANEOUS EQUATIONS             1|SIMULTANEOUS EQUATIONS
 2|1st equation                       2|1st equation
 3|x value  y value  = number        3|x value  y value  = number
 4| 3        2         17             4|    3        2         17
 5|2nd equation                       5|2nd equation
 6|x value  y value  = number        6|x value  y value  = number
 7| 5       -3         22             7|    5       -3         22
 8|                                   8|
 9| A7*A4    A7*B4     A7*C4          9|   15       10         85
10| A4*A7    A4*B7     A4*C7         10|   15       -9         66
11| A9-A10   B9-B10    C9-C10        11|    0       19         19
12|          y =  C11/B11            12|          y =          1
13|          x =  (C4-B4*C12)/A4     13|          x =          5
```

PART TEN

Command
and function
summary

■ SECTION 51
Command summary

All commands have the same basic structure. The simplest form consists of:

/**Command** (minimum data)

Press RETURN at that stage for the basic command, or press ''comma'' to use the command's options.

Options are selected by their initial. Where there are several levels of options, pressing RETURN will terminate the command; pressing ''comma'' will allow another option to be used.

In the summary:

(cell)　　means individual cell.
　　　　　RETURN will select the current cell.

(range)　　means range of cells; either individual cell, whole or partial row, column or block.

(*)　　　　means graph or range of graphs.

(filename) means name of spreadsheet file.
　　　　　ESC will select the current file.
　　　　　RETURN will access the Directory

Housekeeping commands

/**Blank,** (range or * graph range)
　　deletes the contents of a range of cells or graphs.

/**Copy,** (From range),(To cell)
　　duplicates a range in another part of the sheet. Values are　　combined with existing ones in consolidation.
Options **N**o adjust
　　　　Ask for adjust
　　　　Values only
　　　　+ − * / for consolidation

/**Delete,Row,**(number range)
/**Delete,Column,**(letter range)
/**Delete,File,**(filename)
　　removes a slice from the spreadsheet and closes up the gap, or erases a file from the disk.

/**Edit,** (From cell)
　　brings the contents of a cell into the Entry line for Editing before transfer to the current cell.

194

Command summary

/Insert,Row,(number range)
/Insert,Column,(letter range)
    moves rows down or columns right to open space for new ones.

/Move,Row, (From number range),(To number)
/Move,Column, (From letter range),(To letter)
    transfers whole rows or columns from one part of the spreadsheet to another, with automatic adjustment of formula.

/Protect,(range)
    prevents erasure or alteration of cell contents.

/Quit,
    exits from SuperCalc3 − direct to next program if wished.
Options **Yes**
       No
       To (program name)

/Replicate,(From range),(To range)
    creates multiple copies of cell or range of cells.
Options **No** adjust
       Ask for adjust
       Values only
       + − * / for consolidation

/Unprotect,(range)
    removes the protection from the given range.

/Zap,
    deletes the current spreadsheet and user-defined format table.
Options **Yes**
       No
       Contents only retaining Format table

Presentation commands

/Format,Global,
/Format,Row,(number range)
/Format,Column,(letter range)
/Format,Entry,(cell or partial range)
    specifies area for which presentation options are to be given.

■ SECTION 51
Command summary

Options **I**nteger
        General − best fit
        Exponential
        $ − money values
        Right justified numbers
        Left justified numbers
        Text **R**ight justified
        Text **L**eft justified
        * − asterisk bar display
        Hide contents
        User-defined format (number 0 − 9)
        (number 0 − 127) set width
Any combination of options may be used in one command.

/Format,Define
calls up the user-defined format table. Use the cursor keys to move through the table to alter settings, and exit by pressing **F2**.

/Title,Horizontal lock
/Title,Vertical lock
/Title,Both lock
creates fixed titles or headings on the current row and above, or the current column and left.

/Title,Clear removes all locks

/Window,Horizontal
/Window,Vertical
splits the screen at the current row or column and inserts new border.

/Window,Synchronise
links both windows so that they scroll together in the direction of the split.

/Window,Unsynchronise
unlinks the scroll

/Window,Clear
restores whole screen display

Input/output

/eXecute,(filename)
loads in a command file − one with a .XQT ending − and passes each of its lines in turn to the Entry line for execution.

196

■ SECTION 51
Command summary

/Load,(filename),**All**
/Load,(filename),**Part,** (From range),(To range)
/Load,(filename),**Consolidate**
/Load,(filename).*(From graph range), (To number)
Options **N**o adjust
   Ask for adjust
   Values only
   + − * / for consolidation
  Options may only be used with Load...Part.

Output,Display/Contents,(range),Console
Output,Display/Contents,(range),Printer
■ print spreadsheet or list of cell contents on printer or screen.

Output,Display/Contents,(range),Setup,
Options **L**ength of lines
   Width in number of characters
   Auto Form Feed toggle
   Double space toggle
   Setup (printer control codes)
   Print

Output,Display/Contents,(range),Disk,(filename)
  saves spreadsheet or cell contents as text file.

/Save,(filename),**All**
/Save,(filename),**Values only**
/Save,(filename),**Part,All/Values,**(range)
  In both **/Output** and **/Save** commands, if a filename exists, these options will be offered.
   Change name
   Backup
   Overwrite

Graph commands

/View,Data (range)
  selects range for graphing

/View,Graph-type,...
   Pie
   Bar
   Stacked Bar
   Line
   Hi-Lo
   Area

197

■ SECTION 51
Command summary

/View,Time-labels (range)
  selects range for use as labels on horizontal axis

/View,Variable-labels (range)
  selects range for use as labels on legend

/View,Point-labels (range)
  selects range for use as labels on points or tops of bars

/View,Headings,..
  Main,(cell)
  Sub,(cell)
  X-axis,(cell)
  Y-axis,(cell)

/View,Options,Format..
  Axis labels
  Time labels
  Variable labels
  Point labels
  %-pie segment percentages
This option leads on to the normal Format command options.

/View,Options,Explosion,..
  All segments highlighted
  None
  (number 1 – 8) – selected numbers only

/View,Options,Pie-Mode,..
  One Variable,(letter A – J)
  All Variables,(number 1 – 254) – one element from each

/View,Options,Scaling,..
  X-axis
  Y-axis
then specify min and max cells, and number of divisions on scale.

Global commands

/Global,Formula
  toggles display of formula or values

/Global,Next
  toggles automatic cursor movement after ''return''

/Global,Border
  toggles display of row numbers and column letters

■ SECTION 51
Command summary

/Global,Tab
   toggles use of Tab key for moving cursor over blank cells

/Global,Row/Column
   selects order of calculation

/Global,Manual/Auto
   selects manual (on !) or automatic recalculation

/Global,Graphics,...
   Colours − sets pen colours on plotter
   Fonts − selects fonts on plotter
   Layout − sets page size and graph layout on printer or plotter
   Options − leads to Graphics and Device menu
   Install − resets use of memory and screen
   Save − saves program file with current Global Graphics settings

Data management

//Data management,Input,(range)
   defines range that contains records

//Data management,Criterion,(range)
   defines range that contains search criteria

//Data management,Output,(range)
   defines range in which extracted records will be copied

//Data management,Find
   searches for records that match criteria. When found, offers ...
   ↑ − move to next record
   ↓ − move back to previous record
   → − move cursor to field on right
   ← − move cursor to field on left
   return − exit from search

//Data management,Extract
   searches for matching records and copies them to Output range

//Data management,Select
   searches for matching records. When found, offers...
   Yes − copy record to Output
   No − do not copy to Output
   → − move cursor to field on right

   ← − move cursor to field on left
   return − exit from search

■ SECTION 52
Function summary

Introduction

The values in functions may be given directly as numeric, date or text values or constant; or indirectly through cell or range references.

Functions may contain other functions.

Any functional expressions that contain errors will be treated as text.

Functions are limited to a maximum length of 116 characters.

Arithmetic operators and functions

Operators

Arithmetic
+ addition
− subtraction
* multiplication
/ division
^ exponentiation
% percentage of

Relational
= equal to
< less than
> greater than
<= less than or equal to
>= greater than or equal to
<> not equal to

Arithmetic functions

ABS(value) absolute value, ignoring negative

EXP(value) exponent to base e; inverse of **LN**

INT(value) integer, ignoring any decimal part

LN(value) natural logarithm in base e

LOG or **LOG10** logarithm in base 10

MOD(val1,val2) remainder from integer division

ROUND(val1,val2) rounds val1 to val2 decimal places

SQRT(value) square root

Statistical functions

AV or **AVERAGE**(range) mean value of range

COUNT(range) number of cells in range containing values

MAX(range) highest value in range

■ SECTION 52
Function summary

MIN(range) lowest value in range

SUM(range) total of values in range

In this set a (range) may be a list of ranges separated by commas, e.g. SUM(B4:B15,C4:C15,F4:F15).

Trigonometric functions

PI is a constant value, correct to 15 decimal places.

COS(angle) gives the cosine of the angle
SIN(angle) gives the sine of the angle
TAN(angle) gives the tangent of the angle

ACOS (value) inverse of **COS**
ASIN (value) inverse of **SIN**
ATAN (value) inverse of **TAN**

SuperCalc3's functions assume that angles are in radians, where 2*PI radians are equal to 360 degrees. To convert angles in degrees to radians, multiply by PI/180. Thus

   30 degrees = .52359878 Radians

To convert angles in radians into degrees, multiply by 180/PI:

   0.52359878*180/PI = 30

If you prefer to work in degrees, use the trigonometric functions in this form:

   SIN(angle*PI/180) − the angle is entered in degrees

   (ACOS(value))*180/PI − the result is given in degrees

Logical functions

TRUE a constant with a numeric value of 1.

FALSE a constant with a numeric value of 0.

IF(condition,expression-if-true,expression-if-false)

The 'expressions' may be values or functions − including other IF functions. IF the stated condition is TRUE, then the first expression is evaluated and the result displayed in the cell; otherwise the second expression will be used.

Function summary

AND(condition1,condition2)

Both conditions must be true for the function to give a TRUE value.

OR(condition1,condition2)

If either or both conditions are true, then the function will return a TRUE value.

NOT(expression)

Evaluates to FALSE if the expression is true,and vice versa.

Date functions

The three figures needed for a **date value** – month,day,year – may be held in three separate cells, or in a single cell with the functions **DATE** or **TODAY**.

DATE(month,day,year) checks and converts to valid date value if necessary.

TODAY reads the current date from the Amstrad's calendar.

DAY(date value) gives the day of the month.

WDAY(date value) gives the day of the week, with Sunday being shown as 1. To convert this to a day name, a LOOKUP table should be used.

MONTH(date value) gives the month number from a date value. Use a LOOKUP table to convert to month names.

YEAR(date value) gives the year of the date value.

JDATE(date value) converts a date value into the number of days since 1 March 1900.

DVAL(value) inverse of JDATE, converts a number into a date value.

Financial functions

FV(Amount,Interest rate,Periods) gives the future value of a regular saving at a fixed rate.

NPV(Discount rate,range) – initial investment gives the Net Present Value of an investment, based on the returns after discounting for the cost of capital.

■ SECTION 52
Function summary

PV(Amount,Interest rate,Periods) gives the Present Value of a regular return over a number of periods, after discounting.

PMT(Capital,Interest rate,Periods)gives the regular payment needed to repay a loan over a fixed term.

Other functions

LOOKUP(cell,range) finds a matching numeric value in a range and returns the value in the cell to the right of a column range, or below a row range.

NA Not Applicable — displays as **N/A** may be written into a cell to prevent ERROR messages occurring. Used where data is not yet available, or cannot be computed.

ERROR is displayed where essential data or cell references are missing.

ISDATE(cell) returns TRUE value if cell contains date value.

ISTEXT(cell) returns TRUE value if cell contains text.

ISNUM(cell) returns TRUE value if cell contains numeric value or formula.

ISERROR(cell) returns TRUE value if cell contains ERROR.

ISNA(cell) returns TRUE value if cell contains N/A.

Index

Index

Index